Cornell International Industrial and Labor Relations Report Number 12

SOCIAL PARTNERSHIP

The Austrian System of Industrial Relations and Social Insurance

Theodor Tomandl
Karl Fuerboeck

ILR Press
New York State School of
Industrial and Labor Relations
Cornell University

Cover design: Kathleen Dalton

Library of Congress number: 85-14344
ISBN: 0-87546-116-6

Library of Congress Cataloging in Publication Data
Tomandl, Theodor.
Social partnership.
(Cornell international industrial and labor
relations reports ; no. 12)
Bibliography: p.
Includes index.
1. Industrial relations—Austria. 2. Social
security—Austria. I. Fuerboeck, Karl. II. Title.
III. Series: Cornell international industrial and
labor relations reports ; no. 12.
HD8411.T66   1986   331′.09436   85-14344
ISBN 0-87546-116-6

Copies may be ordered from
ILR Press
New York State School of
Industrial and Labor Relations
Cornell University
Ithaca, New York 14851-0952

Printed by Edwards Brothers in the United States of America
5   4   3   2   1

CONTENTS

CONTENTS

TABLES

PREFACE

Since the latter part of the nineteenth century, Austria has made strenuous efforts to tackle the social problems that stemmed from the Industrial Revolution. She has in part availed herself of methods used by neighboring industrial countries, but in some important respects she has gone her own entirely independent way. In her handling of industrial relations and social security issues, Austria has achieved a measure of success.

Austria learned a lesson from her bitter experience during the interwar period and since 1945. She has developed pragmatic ways of dealing with economic, social, and, at least in part, political problems. These have become known far beyond the frontiers of the country by the collective description "social partnership." The social partnership has brought internal stability in party politics and virtually complete freedom from strikes and lockouts. The ability to settle even serious conflicts of interest by peaceful means has enabled the Austrian government, as well as other political and economic forces in the country, to concentrate its attention on the improvement of working conditions and on the consolidation and extension of the social security system. By international comparison, labor standards and social benefits are extremely high in Austria. The social partnership has even allowed the country to weather the economic crisis of the early 1980s largely unscathed.

Yet in non-German-speaking countries little is known of Austria's industrial relations and several social security schemes; this book is intended to fill the regrettable hiatus in knowledge about Austria's industrial relations. It is addressed to readers living outside the German cultural sphere who are accustomed to systems of law rather different from the one in which the authors grew up. If, through this book, we succeed in familiarizing non-Austrian readers with the Austrian political, social, and economic scene, we share credit for the achievement with our translator, Walter Rhodes, and our editor, Roger Haydon. We are also indebted for support and numerous valuable comments and suggestions to Frances Benson, Kurt L. Hanslowe, Wilhelm Meisel, and Robert S. Summers.

We are both trained jurists, and this book is in part a legal work. Nevertheless, we have tried to address economic, political, and social matters to an extent one does not find in Austrian legal treatises. Rather than cramming the book with detail, we have tried to adumbrate in broad outline the principles underlying industrial relations and the system of social security in Austria. We show, further, how those principles are translated into practice.

The book was conceived jointly by the two authors, and we both accept responsibility for it. Such responsibility notwithstanding, chapters 1, 2, and 3 were in the main written by Tomandl, while chapters 4 and 5 were principally Fuerboeck's. The final chapter we wrote together.

Theodor Tomandl
Karl Fuerboeck
Vienna

1

◇

MODERN AUSTRIA

WHEN THE DUAL MONARCHY OF AUSTRIA-HUNGARY collapsed in the aftermath of World War I, what remained of its German-speaking territory became a small country about whose continued existence many observers of the time professed doubt. Yet subsequent events did not bear out their pessimistic forecasts. Austria miraculously survived not only economic depression but also occupation, first by Nazi Germany and then, after 1945, by the four Allied powers. She finally reemerged as an independent state, a federal republic whose institutions were based on models of a distinctly Western stripe. Austria proclaimed permanent neutrality in 1955. A Western-style democracy located on the very doorstep of such eastern bloc countries as Czechoslovakia and Hungary, and of another communist though nonaligned nation, Yugoslavia, she has tried since World War II to play the role of mediator between East and West.

In this country of not quite 84,000 square kilometers, about the size of South Carolina, live 7.5 million people. Forty-two of every hundred inhabitants are gainfully employed, thirty-five of them as wage earners.

The other seven are either self-employed or help in the management of a family business. Of the employed, 10.6 percent are engaged in agriculture and forestry; seven-eights of this group are self-employed or related to the owner of the business. The proportion of women in the working population, almost 39 percent in 1979, continues to rise, so that in 1982 a little more than 50 percent of the white-collar and almost 30 percent of the blue-collar work force were women; only in the public sector is the proportion of women notably smaller, about 21 percent. Women as a group earn markedly less than men do, not because they are paid at lower rates for the same work but rather because most women hold low-paying jobs and because their chances of promotion are not as good as those of men.

Austria is a highly industrialized country. Over the years, agricultural production has fallen to less than 5 percent of the gross national product, in which service industries take pride of place. The service sector also employs the largest proportion of the domestic labor force. The country's economic structure is outlined in table 1.1.

Small- and medium-size enterprises predominate in the Austrian economy. Even if one disregards the agricultural sector, where the number of family establishments has always been exceptionally high, a remarkable 30 percent of all industrial and commercial units are family establishments that employ no outside labor. Furthermore, 78 percent of the remaining businesses employ no more than nine persons. The total number of employees in such firms makes up only one-sixth of the country's working population. Another quarter of them work in firms employing between twenty and one hundred people. Indeed, in 1976

TABLE 1.1

The Economic Structure of Austria, 1982

Economic Sector	Share of Gross Domestic Product (1982 market prices)	Share of Total Employment (July 1982)
Primary	4.3%	1.9%
Secondary	38.2	41.6
Tertiary	53.7	56.5

Source: *Jahrbuch der oesterreichischen Wirtschaft 1982* (Vienna: Bundeskammer der gewerblichen Wirtschaft, 1982), pp. 6, 18.

Notes: The primary sector comprises agriculture, mining, and quarrying, including petroleum and natural gas extraction. The secondary sector, by share of gross domestic product, includes industry (20.2%); construction (7.6%); and energy and water supply (3.7%). The tertiary sector, by share of gross domestic product, includes trade (16.9%); transport (5.7%); and public service (13.3%).

TABLE 1.2

Size of Work Force in

Industrial and Commercial Enterprises, 1976

Size of Enterprise (number of employees)	Number of Enterprises (% of total)		Number of Employees (% of total)	
1–19	155,963	(92.0%)	460,426	(25.5%)
20–99	11,070	(6.5)	477,168	(24.7)
100–999	2,381	(1.4)	571,954	(31.6)
1,000 +	134	(0.1)	324,405	(18.2)
Total	169,548	(100.0)	1,837,953	(100.0)
	Industrial Enterprises (% of all enterprises)		Number of Employees (% of industrial work force)	
1–19	52.5%		27,357	(4.0%)
20–99	31.3		121,052	(17.5)
100–999	15.0		339,944	(49.2)
1,000 +	1.2		202,111	(29.3)
Total	100.0		690,464	(100.0)

Source: *Jahrbuch der oesterreichischen Wirtschaft 1982* (Vienna: Bundeskammer der gewerblichen Wirtschaft, 1982), p. 34.

only 134 enterprises had more than a thousand persons on their pay-rolls—but they accounted for about 18 percent of the country's total employees. Table 1.2 displays the country's employment structure.

The state owns an extremely large number of enterprises. Utilities (electric power generation as well as the extraction of petroleum and natural gas), most of the public transportation system (railroads, aviation, communications), heavy industries, broadcasting (radio and television), and all major banks are the most important areas of public-sector ownership. The banks, moreover, have extensive holdings in many consumer goods manufacturing firms and service industries. As a result, vast areas of the Austrian economy are indirectly owned by the state.

Most state-owned enterprises are organized in the style of public limited companies (joint stock companies) and operate more or less in the same manner as privately owned businesses, with a minimum of ministerial control and intervention. Only a few undertakings, such as railroads, postal services, and gas works, constitute government departments under the direct management of the public authorities. State administration proper (broadly speaking, that is, the civil service) is, if one disregards the state's economic activities, the biggest employer in Austria. No fewer than 540,000 people, almost one-fifth of the total working population, work for the state.

AUSTRIAN POLITICS

Austria is a tightly knit state, composed of nine provinces. There is one federal legislature (consisting of two chambers) and the federal government, on the one hand, and nine provincial, unicameral parliaments and provincial governments, on the other. Legislative and executive powers are distributed between the central and the provincial authorities. For example, labor relations and social insurance fall within the exclusive jurisdiction of federal legislation, whereas welfare and public assistance are provincial matters. This distribution of powers occasionally causes problems. It has, for instance, prevented the establishment of a uniform and financially sound hospital system. It also makes it impossible to replace the current social insurance system with a federal arrangement funded entirely by tax revenues or to introduce uniform federal rules in the area of public assistance.

Despite these various tensions between the provincial and the national levels, the political scene in Austria is marked by an astonishingly high degree of stability. The unwritten rules of the political game, vital to the proper functioning of a democracy, are scrupulously observed by all the major political forces in the country. The Roman Catholic church, to which the vast majority of Austrians adhere, has withdrawn completely from party politics. Parliamentary and local elections seldom produce major changes in the respective strengths of the major political parties. The Socialist party and the moderately conservative Austrian People's party represent the dominant political forces, and only one further political grouping is represented in Parliament, the Austrian Freedom party, whose ideology mixes old-style liberalism and a mild form of pan-Germanism. Since the 1959 elections the Communist party has not won a single seat in Parliament and has virtually ceased to be a political force of any weight in Austria.

Until 1966 Austria was ruled by a coalition government formed by the Socialist and the People's parties. In that year the People's party won the election and formed a government on its own. The Socialists won an absolute majority in 1971 and held power for a dozen years, with the People's party relegated to the role of loyal opposition. In 1983 the Socialists lost their absolute majority and formed a coalition government with the Freedom party.

Although it has been out of power at the federal level for well over a decade, the People's party is still a potent political force. In six of Austria's nine provinces the People's party holds the majority of seats in the provincial parliament and thus nominates the provincial governors, who usually head the provincial government. Certain legislative and, to a limited extent, taxing powers are vested in the provinces. Thus, despite the political preponderance of the central government, the federal authorities must establish a measure of consensus with the provincial governments.

THE AUSTRIAN LEGAL SYSTEM

The law and the concept of legality occupy an extraordinarily elevated position in the minds of Austrians, to an extent that may seem incomprehensible to foreign observers. For many years strenuous efforts have been made to democratize and bring within the scope of the law more and more aspects of human existence and aspiration. These endeavors have indelibly stamped the society. Legislation is readily used as a means of changing the structure of society and of enforcing new standards of conduct and notions of value. To understand how social policies are framed and implemented, some knowledge of the basic concepts of Austrian law is necessary, especially as the administration of the state is mostly in the hands of lawyers.

At the summit of the Austrian legal body is the Austrian Constitution, a document enacted by Parliament in 1920 and frequently amended since. The constitution contains directly enforceable legal provisions rather than political programs to be executed by government. A special court, the Constitutional High Court, is exclusively charged with safeguarding the rules and civil rights protected by the constitution. The Constitutional High Court alone may invalidate (declare unconstitutional) statutes or regulations. Details of the constitution may be modified or repealed with the consent of two-thirds of the members of the lower chamber of Parliament, the National Council; more fundamental changes also require a referendum. Hence the political agendas of the major political parties are limited by the constitution, because to change constitutional norms they need to cooperate with one another. In this way the constitution provides one of the bases for Austria's peculiar political stability.

Under the provisions of the constitution, the executive function, both at the federal and at the provincial levels, is subordinate to the legislature. The power to legislate is thus of particular importance. Any executive interference in the rights and interests of the citizen must derive its authority, clearly and explicitly, from a statute passed by the legislature. Lacking such authority, executive decisions may be set aside by the Constitutional High Court or the Administrative High Court.

At the national level, the right to legislate is vested in the two chambers of the Parliament, the National Council and the Federal Council. The latter, generally considered to represent the provinces, has limited powers: it can only suspend, but not revoke, legislation passed by the lower chamber. Since 1959 only three political parties have gained seats in the National Council, where party discipline is quite strictly enforced.

Both members of Parliament and the federal government have the right to initiate legislation, but in practice the government is responsible for most of the bills that eventually find their way into the statute book. Private members' bills are exceedingly rare. Political parties and politicians are generally content to set down in broad outline the principles and purposes that legislation is intended to realize. Thereafter, the departmental bureaucracies will normally cooperate with the major organizations representing both sides of industry to determine the form and content of legislation.

Major interest groups exert influence on the framing of legislation at three different stages. Before the department concerned drafts a government bill, it normally holds extensive consultations with the interest groups and sometimes with other agencies (the provincial governments, other departments) interested in the subject matter of the proposed bill. After this preliminary round of negotiations, the department prepares the official draft of the bill, which it submits to these same organizations for their comments. The draft, once suitably amended, will be submitted to Parliament as a government bill, to be enacted in due form and passed into law. In Parliament, each major interest group can rely for support on the deputies who are its members; such deputies and experts, provided by the groups to help the bill through committee, allows the interest organizations a third opportunity to make their influence felt in the process of legislation.

The practice of submitting proposed legislation to interested parties before any formal parliamentary consideration has much to recommend it. It offers the best chance of reaching compromise on controversial issues and securing consent for proposed laws. And it is effective: the majority of legal enactments, after a phase of stiff bargaining, are adopted with the consent of all three political parties in Parliament.

Under the terms of the constitution, acts of Parliament (and regulations made by the executive under the authority of such acts) are the only source of law; the courts may not overstep the boundaries that legislation sets. But in practice, the difference from so-called common-law countries is not as striking as theory would suggest. Austrian legislation establishes general rules and then introduces separate legal provisions, sometimes in considerable detail, to flesh out those rules and thus confer precision and clarity upon them. Nevertheless, the courts frequently confront situations that the legislators had not foreseen, where the language of the legislation is ambiguous, or where laws and rules clash with the provisions of other enactments. In such cases, judges frequently establish new legal rules and norms. The actual power of the judiciary to refine existing laws in this inconspicuous manner, often to a point where a new law emerges, is of particular importance in labor law.

The Austrian Constitution clearly distinguishes between private and public law. In private law, individual persons are permitted, autonomously and on the basis of absolute equality, to regulate their mutual relations in any manner they choose. The law confines itself, first and foremost, to establishing the conditions required for the exercise of these autonomous rights, to redressing imbalances in the negotiating strengths of the parties, and to providing the necessary sanctions and means of enforcement. Property law and the law of contract (of which labor law, at least its essential features, is a part) constitute the nucleus of private law. In contrast, public law is marked by inequality between the parties it affects: the state, represented by a host of public authorities, on the one hand, and the individual citizen on the other. In the relationship between the state and the individual, the latter is clearly subordinate to the former. Public law concerns itself with the machinery of government and with the manner in which the relations between the state (or any other unit wielding a measure of sovereign power) and the citizen are to be regulated. Examples of public law include social insurance law and the law relating to public assistance. The practical significance of this distinction lies in the different constitutional status of the officials who are called upon to administer these two branches of the law. Disputes in private law are settled by the judiciary (under the terms of the constitution independent of both the legislature and the executive). The officials who administer public law, however, enjoy no such constitutionally guaranteed independence.

One further difference deserves to be noted: private law consists of comparatively few legal provisions. These provisions are mostly of a permissive nature in that they nearly always give way to the contrary intentions of the parties. The number of legal enactments and regulations in the field of public law is, however, very high and increases year by year. Moreover, the provisions of public law strictly circumscribe the manner in which the authorities are allowed to proceed.

Occasionally, the two types of law overlap and blend into each other. The state, as owner of property, is entitled to enter into contractual relationships with individual persons and legal entities. In social insurance law, some provisions belong to the sphere of private law; conversely, labor law contains several rules that have to be classified as public law. The government, in order to free itself of the shackles of constitutional convention, will even use the devices and possibilities that private law puts at the disposal of individuals. For example, in 1971, the federal government brought in a bill designed to use revenues from public taxation to compensate crime victims for bodily injuries. Such compensation is in theory exclusively a matter for the provinces, but they did not have the funds necessary to implement the scheme and would probably not have produced a uniform national scheme. To get the required legislation enacted at the federal level, Parliament used the medium of private law, enacting a statute that obliged the government to compensate the victims of serious crimes with state property. (Under private law, the government as property owner can dispose of its property as it wishes.)

The executive and the judiciary are constitutionally separate. The validity of a decision made by an administrative authority may not be contested in a court of law, and conversely the judgment of a court cannot be appealed before an administrative authority. The only exceptions that the constitution allows are the Constitutional High Court and the Administrative High Court, two public-law courts that exercise a measure of control over the state administration. The jurisdiction of the Administrative High Court may only be invoked after all administrative appeals have been exhausted and even then only on certain specified grounds. Moreover, a complaint may only be brought on a point of law; the facts as established by the administrative authority cannot be challenged before the court. These rules appear to be cut and dried; but a stratagem has been devised in some areas of administration whereby a party aggrieved by the decision of an administrative authority can bring proceedings before an ordinary court of civil law. The mere institution of such proceedings automatically suspends the contested decision until the court has considered the matter. This stratagem has been used in social insurance law.

One further constitutional aspect is worth mentioning. The constitution enshrines both human and civic rights; their protection is entrusted to the Constitutional High Court. Fundamental rights secure to each individual a defined sphere of strict privacy, free from state interference—but the catalogue of constitutionally guaranteed rights includes no social rights calculated to secure specified state action for the benefit of the individual citizen. "Social rights," such as the right to work or the right to education, would constitute a social program, which in Austria is reserved to the legislature.

Of constitutionally guaranteed rights, the principle of equality has proved to be of great importance in matters of social policy; the principle of equality is enshrined in the constitution and therefore cannot be abolished through ordinary legislation. The principle is, in an important sense, binding on the legislature. The Constitutional High Court occasionally declares laws and regulations invalid on the basis of these guaranteed rights, though it cannot reformulate offending articles. For example, the court, in a renowned judgment, ruled in 1980 that the manner in which social insurance law treated widows and widowers was incompatible with the constitutionally guaranteed principle of equality between the sexes and repealed the offending passages in the legislation. The finding forced the government to introduce new legislation designed to regulate benefits in a constitutionally acceptable manner. The principle of equality is also binding upon the parties to a collective agreement. In private law, on the other hand, the parties to a contract can establish their relations in any way they choose. Fundamental rights can be invoked to revise a contract only under most unusual circumstances. The principle of nondiscrimination can be observed, nevertheless, in labor law, particularly in requirements that employers do not arbitrarily discriminate among members of their work forces.

International law also affects national law relating to labor relations and social security. Austria has ratified numerous international agreements and conventions promulgated by the International Labour Organisation, the United Nations, and the Council of Europe. These instruments, however, are seldom "self-executing" in the sense that the courts can directly apply them. Thus Austria, when signing an international agreement, will usually reserve the right to discharge her obligations by enacting appropriate domestic legislation. This procedure is also required because in many instances domestic legislation provides benefits that already exceed the standards that the international agreements are trying to establish.

AUSTRIAN LAW AND THE CITIZEN

Austrians are rightly proud of the way in which justice is dispensed in the country. It is possible to bring a legal action with a minimum of formality, and a litigant will not, as a rule, need the services of a lawyer, at least in the court of first instance. In trials involving the application of labor or social insurance law, for instance, litigants are usually assisted and represented by officials of the employers' and employees' organizations experienced in the relevant branch of the law. Such legal advice and representation are provided to the litigant free of charge. Appeals go to the court of second instance, with usually a further appeal on legal points to the court of third and last instance. At the top of this hierarchy of civil courts is the Supreme Court, whose judgment cannot be appealed.

Judges in Austria are appointed for life and hold office "during good behavior," subject to a mandatory retirement age. In order to safeguard their independence, judges cannot be removed from a position or transferred to another post without their agreement. In their judicial capacity, they are subject neither to governmental direction nor to the control of a court, except by way of appeal.

Civil actions are, in principle, tried by professional judges without a jury. In trials involving the application of labor or social insurance law, however, the bench includes lay assessors who join with the professional judges to render judgment. Free legal aid, including the services of a lawyer when necessary, is available to impecunious litigants, who are also excused from payment of court costs.

Persons who feel themselves injured by an administrative decree are entitled to contest it by appeal to a higher administrative authority, often with the possibility of a further appeal to the top of the administrative hierarchy. After all administrative appeals are exhausted, the aggrieved party may invoke the jurisdiction of the Administrative High Court on a point of law, asking that the court set aside a given decree on the grounds that it is at variance with the law or that the authority that

practiced in Austria during the "Great Coalition" of the People's party and the Socialist party, from 1945 to 1966, and also thereafter when governments were formed by single parties—the People's party from 1966 to 1970, the Socialist party from 1970 to 1983. Even during the single-party era, the social partners frequently managed to prevent the government from adopting extreme measures on controversial matters.

No elaborate philosophy underpins the system of social partnership. Rather, the system reflects the general, received views of those who participate in it. And the fact that the specific aims pursued by each of the partners frequently diverge has not hurt the system. For, as an Organization for Economic Cooperation and Development (OECD) report of 1981 accurately notes, Austrians are in fundamental agreement about the need to settle conflicts and wield power in a spirit of moderation and cooperation.

In Austria voluntary interest organizations are formed as associations. The Austrian Association Act is an exceedingly liberal and permissive statute, and the government refrains from interfering in the work of associations as long as they do not pursue unlawful objectives. Because of these permissive circumstances, trade unions and other groups have generally organized themselves as associations.

But voluntary associations are only half the story. One peculiarity of the Austrian scene is that political and social forces erect statutory bodies, whose appointed task it is to represent the economic interests of their members. These are the so-called chambers. A chamber, like an association, has its own legal identity; unlike an association, however, it is a creature of statutory law in the sense that it owes its existence to a particular legal enactment, which in turn determines its objectives and its internal organization. Furthermore, membership is obligatory for all those whose economic interests the chamber was established to represent: no qualified member may resign or be excluded or expelled from his or her chamber.

The chamber is an autonomous body run by its members, who elect its officers. All chambers are empowered to levy from their members contributions that, within limits defined by statute, they are entitled to fix. However, chambers, unlike associations, are subject to a measure of state control, for the state can rescind chamber decisions that are at variance with law. Indeed, some chamber decisions, in order to be valid, must be endorsed by public authority. In practice, though, the authorities seldom if ever interfere in the internal arrangements of a chamber.

The various chambers are intended to afford persons engaged in industrial, commercial, and agricultural activities, as well as in the liberal professions (e.g., medical practitioners, architects, pharmacists, lawyers), on the one hand, and workers, on the other, the opportunity to define and defend their common economic interests. The chambers have thus come to be regarded by the government as issue-specific partners, and historical analysis helps reveal the developing nature of the partnership.

A Brief History of the Partnership

The foundations of the Austrian system of social partnership are the employers' organizations and those representing the interests of employees. The country's organizational scheme, where voluntary associations exist side by side with chambers in which membership is compulsory for all in a given trade or vocation, dates back to the nineteenth century. The development of trade unions was of decisive importance. It was only after the removal of the ban on workers' combinations in 1867, and after strikes ceased to be punishable offenses in 1870, that trade unionism in the form of voluntary associations began to spread in Austria. The early unions were purely local in character, and they operated in limited industrial areas. Later, these unions coalesced into larger units, and it became evident that political orientations were determining the character of the new associations and commanding the loyalty of their members. The turn of the century saw the emergence of three large groups of trade unions, each with a markedly different ideological outlook. Groups voicing the political views of Socialists, Christian Socials, and pan-German Nationalists competed fiercely for support among the working classes.

Employers were not slow to react to the growing union movement. They closed ranks and also formed voluntary employers' associations. These originally operated on a purely local basis, but later they also merged into larger units, which tended to represent various regional or sectoral interests rather than a clear-cut political ideology.

From the mid-nineteenth century employers had the benefit of a second forum that represented their interests: the chambers of commerce, which were created by statutory law. The chambers of commerce became generally recognized as representatives of industry. Their importance and prestige were greatly enhanced when they obtained the right to designate a number of members of Parliament. The chambers were not, however, concerned with labor relations as such, since the working class had not yet gained the parliamentary franchise. Workers agitated in vain for similar chambers that would protect and represent workers' interests and, above all, secure them a measure of parliamentary representation.

It was not until the collapse of the monarchy and the establishment of the Austrian Republic that the working class realized these aspirations. In each of the nine provinces of which the new federal state was composed, one chamber of labor was established. Membership in these chambers became obligatory for practically all wage earners. By this time the working class had obtained the right to vote in parliamentary elections and was represented in Parliament by the Social Democratic party. Thus it was the coordination rather than the pursuit of political aims that became the main function of the newly formed chambers of labor. Like the chambers of commerce, they did not concern themselves with collective agreements.

From 1933 to 1938, after the so-called self-elimination of Parliament, the government, composed of nominees of the Christian Socials, sought to restructure state and society after the pattern of the medieval "corporate" system *(Staendestaat)*, with its peculiar brand of checks and balances. As a corollary, the government banned all other political parties and suppressed the three existing trade union movements, replacing them with a single, and compliant, union. The German invasion, followed shortly thereafter by the complete absorption of Austria into the German Reich, ended this experiment. Austrian politicians and trade union leaders, who in the past had exhibited little taste for cooperation, shared common experiences either as comrades in arms in the German military or as fellow sufferers in the concentration camps. Personal contacts thus forged among these former political adversaries later proved to be of cardinal importance.

After Austria's liberation in 1945, surviving trade union leaders decided not to reestablish rival union movements. Even before the Austrian state was officially reestablished, the Austrian Federation of Trade Unions (*Oesterreichischer Gewerkschaftsbund,* or OGB) was formed as a politically neutral association that was to transcend party lines and be open to adherents of all political and religious creeds. In point of fact, the Allied occupation authorities allowed only three political parties to operate in postwar Austria: in order of electoral strength, the People's party, the Socialist party, and the Communist party. The nominees of these parties cooperated in managing the newly created OGB, and the principle of a national trade union movement has survived to this day.

On the employers' side, the chambers of commerce survived the Nazis and the war; after 1945 they were purged of National Socialist elements. Since then they have added to their traditional activities by assuming the task of representing members' interests in matters of industrial relations. Employers also demonstrated considerable enthusiasm for the formation of new voluntary associations, representing the special economic interests of particular lines of business. The Federation of Austrian Industrialists (*Vereinigung Oesterreichischer Industrieller,* or VOI) is the most important of these new associations. Agricultural chambers, created by statute in each province to represent the special interests of agriculture and forestry, have also gained great importance. In two provinces the agricultural chambers include employees, while special agricultural workers chambers watch over employees' interests in the other seven provinces. Constitutional considerations forbid the creation of a single, central organization to represent the interests of agriculture and forestry at the national (federal) level, and for that reason the agricultural chambers have formed the Presidents' Conference of Austrian Agricultural Chambers to operate at the national level.

None of these organizations is officially linked to a particular political party—indeed, they boast of operating above party lines. But despite their avowed political neutrality, as a practical matter they adopt policies that reflect, at least in part, the political viewpoint of the majority of their members. Thus the OGB and the chambers of labor clearly favor the Socialist party, whereas the chambers of commerce and the agricultural chambers incline toward the People's party. The fact that these four groups represent the economic interests and the political views of the vast majority of Austrians has become the basis of the social partnership.

In 1945 cooperation among these four groups (the OGB and the chambers) was rendered imperative by two pressing problems: the need to rebuild the domestic economy and the presence of the occupying powers. A further problem that encouraged unification did not disappear with the departure of the occupying armies in 1955—inflation. Indeed, it was the challenge of inflation that prompted the four groups in

1947 to set up, on an informal yet permanent basis, the first institutional evidence of the partnership, a joint economic commission. Within the framework of the commission, they then agreed on five pacts dealing with prices and wages. In 1951 the federal government endeavored to turn the joint commission into an official economic directorate, in whose proceedings the government itself would participate. A year later, however, the Constitutional High Court rejected the federal government's attempt.

In 1957, on the joint initiative of Johann Boehm, president of the OGB, and Julius Raab, then federal chancellor and de facto representative of the chamber of commerce, a new venture in social cooperation with government participation was devised, again on an informal, voluntary basis. A gentlemen's agreement established the Joint Commission for Price and Wage Questions. The official designation in German uses the adjective *paritaetische* before the word "Commission." There is no exact equivalent in English; the name implies strict equality among the social partners, as employers and employees are represented on the commission equally. Commission decisions require the unanimous consent of the constituent organizations.

The new joint commission was mainly intended to check the rise in prices and to coordinate wage policies throughout Austria. (Two subcommittees were created to concern themselves with prices and wages.) The joint commission has, however, no power of coercion and no authority to impose sanctions on those who choose to ignore its decisions. Its effectiveness depends entirely on the ability of participating organizations to influence their members to abide by the commission's decisions.

In 1963 the Advisory Council on Economic and Social Questions was established as the third subcommittee of the joint commission. It subjects economic policies that the government is considering to critical analysis and makes recommendations and proposals in regard to these policies on behalf of constituent organizations. Through this advisory council the joint committee transcended its original limits, allowing organizations to take part in the entire process of economic policy making. Indeed, already becoming aware of the interdependence of all aspects of economic development, the various organizations started to supplement their wage and price agreements with similar arrangements on various aspects of national economic policy, such as labor market, fiscal, monetary, and even investment policy.

Organization of Workers

The Austrian Federation of Trade Unions is the most powerful voluntary association in Austria. Widely regarded as one of the most centralized trade union federations in the free world, the OGB, as distinct from its constituent unions, concentrates power because of the way it was originally organized. Under the OGB charter, the fifteen constituent unions have no legal independent identity. They are no more than subordinate agencies of the federation, and de jure it is only on behalf of the federation that they can act (though in practice they proceed under their own names). The federation has the power of the purse, setting membership fees and administering union funds, but it allows the constituent unions a large measure of independence. The individual unions recruit members, for example, even though members are enrolled in the federation and not the recruiting union.

The federation's top management is not directly elected and therefore cannot be removed from office by the rank and file. Various political interests within the federation are represented on its governing boards and committees; the proportions of membership are determined by a compromise arrangement among these interests, with the proviso that due regard will be paid to the results of both works council elections as well as elections of the governing bodies of the chamber of labor. The federation's functionaries are thus appointed from the top down rather than from the bottom up. Although this selection process occasionally provokes criticism from outsiders, the rank and file do not seem to find it objectionable. Membership in the OGB is surprisingly high, some 60 percent of the total Austrian work force. Resignations are rare, and the number of workers who at the behest of the federation take part in industrial actions is usually very high; strikes against the federation's policies are, on the other hand, virtually unknown.

Despite the vast power held by the leaders of the OGB, the fifteen member unions play the most important role in the day-to-day issues facing the union movement. These unions negotiate collective agreements and hence shape Austrian wage policy. All but two of the fifteen are organized along horizontal, or industry-specific, lines. All workers in an industry or a group of kindred industries are eligible for membership in the same union, regardless of the kind of work they perform. For instance, the union representing the work force in the metal and mining industries and power supply (these three industries are grouped together) includes gatekeepers, drivers, toolmakers, and cleaners—indeed, anyone employed by a firm in these industries. Thus the union is able to settle any demarcation disputes—who should perform certain kinds of work—on its own. Although subdivisions exist in each of the unions, these enjoy only a very limited measure of independence.

There are two white-collar unions in Austria: the Union of White-Collar Workers in Private Enterprise, and the union that organizes white-collar workers in the arts, the media, and the so-called liberal professions. These two unions are not organized on an industry-specific basis but rather represent white-collar workers regardless of where they are employed. (The former union is the largest in Austria.) The organizational separation between the two has made it possible for different

TABLE 2.1

Membership in the

Austrian Federation of Trade Unions (OGB)

Union	Number of Union Members	Union Members as Percent of OGB Strength
White-collar workers in private enterprise	345,626	20.8%
Government service*	214,857	12.9
Local government service*	167,020	10.1
Art, media, liberal professions	17,025	1.0
Building, timber industries	190,108	11.5
Chemical industry	60,157	3.6
Railroads*	117,973	7.1
Printing, paper industries	23,124	1.4
Trade, transport, traffic	37,340	2.3
Hotels, catering, personal services	46,809	2.8
Agriculture, forestry	20,005	1.2
Food industry	44,481	2.7
Metal, mining industries, power supply	251,576	18.0
Textiles, clothing, leather	50,772	3.1
Postal, telephone, telegraph	73,580	4.4
Total	1,660,453	100.0

Source: *Arbeit und Wirtschaft* 6(1984):6.

Notes: The total number of union members is 61.4 percent of the Austrian work force.

*Denotes public-service unions.

white-collar interests to be independently represented, and the OGB has thus avoided the creation of new and competing white-collar unions. Four separate unions, all operating under the OGB umbrella, represent the interests of employees in the public service.

No trade unions are based on membership in a particular factory, workshop, or business. Members of unions in a particular establishment may maintain loose contacts with those in others, but such cooperation is not institutionalized. There are no legal or official links of any kind between the trade unions, on the one hand, and the works councils elected to represent the staff of particular firms, on the other.

A chamber of labor (the official designation is the Chamber for Blue-Collar and White-Collar Workers) has been established in each province under the Chambers of Labor Act. Agricultural and forestry workers have their own special chambers; otherwise, membership in the local chamber of labor is obligatory for employees of any description unless they are in public service or occupy key managerial positions in private business. There are no further vocational divisions within the chambers, for in the main these bodies consider questions that interest the working class as a whole.

The nine provincial chambers are linked together in the Austrian Chambers of Labor Conference, which is responsible for dealing with labor problems at the federal level. Although the chambers of labor are empowered to act for their members in the matter of collective agreements, they leave such bargaining entirely to the trade unions. The chambers of labor regard themselves, instead, as the intellectual spearheads of the labor movement and view their principal function as underpinning trade union policies with the necessary scientific data and arguments. The brain trust of the union movement, the chambers publish numerous books and periodicals and also take a keen interest in consumer protection. Like the other chambers, they must be consulted on any government bill that affects their members' interests before the proposed bill may be brought before Parliament. The chambers are represented in numerous government institutions, and on the various boards and committees established within the framework of the country's social security system. The chambers of labor act as the extended arm of the OGB, relieving the federation of responsibility for especially costly activities and assuming those tasks that only a statutory body can manage effectively.

The trade union wings of political parties are not officially repre-

TABLE 2.2

Chambers of Labor Election Results

	1974	1979	1984
Total votes	1,202,876	1,233,251	1,271,847
Participation in election	61.1%	63.4%	63.6%
Voting strength in trade union wing			
Socialist party	64.3	63.4	58.7
People's party	31.0	29.1	36.5
Freedom party	3.2	4.6	2.5
Other*	1.5	2.9	2.3

Source: *Arbeit und Wirtschaft* 9(1979):58, and 6(1984):16.

Note: *Includes Communist Party.

sented on the various boards and committees of the OGB. In the chambers of labor, however, they do compete for seats in the quasi-legislative assemblies that control the chambers' top management. The members of these assemblies are elected along parliamentary lines. Thus the key positions in the chambers of labor are filled by the nominees of the trade unions, who ensure that the chambers follow the policies espoused by the OGB. On the whole, the sharing of tasks between the chambers and the OGB (the latter being the senior partner) has not given rise to serious problems. The legal requirement of membership in the chambers does not seem to have militated against voluntary membership in the unions, even though wage earners in large industrial and commercial enterprises—and most trade union members work in large firms—pay three sets of dues: to the chamber of labor, to the OGB, and to their local works council fund.

ORGANIZATION OF EMPLOYERS

In the case of employees, voluntary organizations dominate the statutory bodies; on the employers' side, the position is clearly reversed: the statutory bodies and, first and foremost, the chambers of commerce eclipse voluntary associations in importance.

The organization of the chambers of commerce is quite complex and may appear to outsiders as unnecessarily cumbersome. (The English translation "chambers of commerce" is inaccurate and misleadingly restrictive, but no phrase translates *Kammer der gewerblichen Wirtschaft* concisely. *Gewerbliche Wirtschaft* includes a self-employed person's pursuit of any industrial or commercial activity other than in agriculture and forestry and the liberal professions.)

There are nine chambers of commerce, one in each province. They include within their six sections—commerce, crafts and industry, transport, tourism, finance, banking and insurance—virtually every area of Austrian free enterprise. All establishments whose activity falls under one of these sections are compulsorily enrolled as members of a chamber and of its subordinate units. The six sections are in turn divided into numerous units, each of which represents the specific interests of a particular branch. These units are called groups *(Fachgruppen)*. The nine provincial chambers are integrated into one central agency, the Federal Chamber of Commerce; but each of the constituent chambers retains its own legal identity.

In organizational terms, the federal chamber mirrors the provincial chambers. There are six sections within the federal chamber, and each is further divided into units known as "combinations" *(Fachverbaende)* rather than "groups." Thus, for example, the owner of a café in Vienna is required by law to be simultaneously a member of the Vienna Catering Trade Group, the Vienna provincial chamber, the Federal Catering Trade Combination, and the federal chamber.

There are historical reasons for this complexity. After World War II, it was decided to integrate the formerly autonomous guilds into the chambers of commerce and to create the federal chamber as an umbrella organization for the operations of the various provincial chambers. This arrangement was adopted so that each branch of industry and commerce could define and voice, at both the provincial and federal levels, its specific claims and grievances. The arrangement also gave rise to a system of checks and balances within the chamber system, which is intended to make sure that the often divergent, and on occasion mutually exclusive, interests of the members can be reconciled and coordinated.

The chambers of commerce, as well as those subunits that have a legal identity of their own, possess the legal capacity to enter into collective agreements on behalf of their members and to represent them in proceedings before the labor courts. On the employers' side they discharge all the functions that the chambers of labor perform in the interests of the wage-earning classes. In addition, the chambers of commerce represent Austrian industry worldwide through a system of trade representatives, a service that only governments offer in other countries.

As membership in the chambers of commerce is obligatory for virtually all individual entrepreneurs, policies that the chambers adopt tend to lay special emphasis on the interests of small- and medium-size undertakings. But difficulties arise from the constant need to reconcile conflicting interests, as well as from the limitations that attend the chambers' status as public bodies superintended by the state. As a result, voluntary entrepreneurs' organizations have been established outside the chamber system. They represent the interests of their members not only vis-à-vis the government and the public but also vis-à-vis the chambers of commerce. Occasionally they manage to get their candidates elected to office within the chamber system. Only a few of these voluntary organizations have shown any inclination to become involved in collective bargaining or, indeed, to concern themselves with industrial relations at all; but those few have effectively supplanted the chamber of commerce in the field concerned.

The OGB and the Federal Chamber of Commerce play the leading roles in the Austrian system of social partnership. None of the other organizations has attained a similar importance, not the agricultural and agricultural workers' chambers nor other chambers of rather minor significance that represent the interests of the liberal professions, such as medical practitioners, pharmacists, architects, lawyers, and notaries. Some of these chambers also concern themselves with the interests of their members' employees. One remaining and major group of employees is not enrolled in a chamber of its own, and indeed in no chamber, namely, civil servants, whose interests are safeguarded exclusively by their trade unions.

How the Social Partnership Works

Austria has never known a statutory income policy imposed by wage and price controls (such as existed in the United States during the Nixon administration and in Britain on several occasions). Nor does the government set up formal price guidelines. Yet the unions have developed an understanding of the need for an efficient investment policy, and all the partners share ideas about the economic limitations on distributable income. This basically conservative orientation of the partners has provoked some criticism, but it has also produced a degree of harmony that seems remarkable when one compares Austria to other Western countries.

Both government and Parliament have seen to it that the major organizations are represented on numerous advisory boards and committees concerned with the formulation of economic and social policy and that their views are heard before final decisions are taken. The organizations are also entitled to nominate lay judges for the labor courts and social insurance arbitration tribunals, and they are duly represented on the governing bodies of the autonomous social insurance carriers. Of greatest significance, however, is the fact that, because of their participation in the work of so many different institutions, the representatives of the four groups (the OGB and the three major chambers) are in constant contact with one another.

It is of vital importance that the top people in these groups frequently meet with one another as well as with the members of the government who are charged with economic affairs and continuously exchange views on points of common interest, obtaining timely information on all important issues. On the strength of this information and their standing within their respective organizations, they can help settle incipient conflicts.

Such a system has its weaknesses. It can work only if the people at the head of the organizations are strong personalities whose standing with their rank and file is beyond challenge and who are wholehearted in their willingness to cooperate with their counterparts in other organizations. Moreover, the phenomenon of "personal union" must be noted. Personal union involves the simultaneous exercise by one and the same person of functions both in one of the organizations and in one of the political parties. For example, Anton Benya, who chairs the OGB, is simultaneously a top figure in the Socialist party and speaker of the lower house of Parliament. Rudolf Sallinger, the president of the Federal Chamber of Commerce, is also a member of Parliament and one of the leaders in the People's party. The fact that these two men, despite the barriers of party politics and class interests, have come to understand and respect each other is of tremendous importance to Austria.

Harmony has achieved more for members of the various organizations than confrontation would have. Cooperation has not precluded organizations from forcibly espousing their own aims and aspirations. But when on the brink of confrontation, leaders have generally decided to opt for cooperation and compromise. On more than one occasion, indeed, the social partners have achieved compromise by passing the buck to the government, forcing the government to solve seemingly intractable problems; for example, inducing the government to grant tax concessions that make a relatively modest wage increase more attractive to the workers concerned. There are even examples of genuine trade-offs to be found: unions, for example, proposing and even insisting on tax reductions in exchange for moderate wage demands.

The practice of the system of social partnership has produced in leaders of the various organizations a sense of their social and economic responsibilities to society as a whole rather than just to the members of their specific organization. It is by no means unusual for functionaries of the employers' organizations to appeal to their members to show restraint in their pricing decisions, and, conversely, for trade union leaders to publicly advocate moderation in wage demands. Social partnership also allows a long-term approach to decision making; for tactical reasons, an organization will often be willing to forgo a short-term benefit for the sake of long-term advantage.

In 1973, for example, the OGB could have given unqualified support to the extreme views of the Socialist government regarding the extent of employees' participation in the management of the businesses in which they worked. Indeed, had the OGB endorsed these views on codetermination it would have increased its own popularity among the workers concerned. The Socialist program had, however, met with the firm opposition of employers. The OGB negotiated a compromise with the employers' organizations, deleting from the government bill in question those passages to which employers had taken the most violent exception. The compromise bill eventually received unanimous parliamentary support. The OGB, through its moderation, ensured that the principal portions of the statute survived partisan change in parliamentary elections.

By patient negotiation, the trade unions have, in the course of the years, succeeded in obtaining better working conditions, higher wages, and extensions of the social security system for their members. Yet these negotiations have made it possible for employers to ward off incursions into particularly sensitive areas of managerial prerogative. The system has also allowed employers to enlist the support of the unions on occasion, and, of course, they have been spared the stresses of industrial unrest. Although there is no consensus among economists as to the immediate effects of the joint commission on wage and price movements in Austria, it is generally conceded that the commission has at least managed to spread price and wage increases over reasonably long periods of time, effectively averting the danger of dramatic and simultaneous increases in prices and wages.

There is no doubt that close cooperation between the social partners is in the government's interest. The social partners settle many conflicts that would otherwise appear on the government's agenda. Yet such powerful partners also constitute a potential threat to government authority. Not only can the partner organizations rely upon the solidarity of their members but their leaders are also members of Parliament and leading figures in the political parties. In these circumstances, a minister depends entirely on his or her charisma and public confidence to carry a point against an organization's opposition. Related problems also arise when the government proposes measures that bear on the interests of those sections of the population that are *not* represented by a powerful organization.

The side-by-side existence of constitutionally defined and de facto power centers has stimulated a good deal of discussion among constitutional lawyers. Yet, while scholars and journalists concentrate on theoretical problems inherent in the social partnership, the spirit of cooperation that manifests itself in the system commands the support of the overwhelming majority of Austrians. The OECD undertook a detailed examination of the Austrian system in 1981, and it concluded that, thanks to the social partnership, economic and social development in Austria had proceeded along lines that were by international standards distinctly favorable. The rate of economic growth had exceeded the average OECD rate, both price increases and nominal wage increases had been below those in the rest of Western Europe, and as a result full employment had been maintained. The Austrian economy has proved itself remarkably resistant.

3

◇

THE LAW OF INDUSTRIAL RELATIONS

AUSTRIAN INDUSTRIAL RELATIONS ARE TO A large extent determined by statutory law enacted by Parliament, and this body of labor law addresses diverse problems. It has become customary to classify legal provisions and other normative rules that make up labor law under the headings of individual and collective labor law.

Individual labor law is concerned with all questions that arise from the relationship between employer and employee; it is therefore a satellite of the law relating to employment contracts, which deals with the formation, the contents, the termination, and, where applicable, the aftereffects of employment contracts. The parties to such contracts are not free to agree to any terms they wish. Most of the legal provisions are compulsory, in the sense that the parties cannot validly contract out of them, unless the arrangement proposed as an alternative is more beneficial to the employee than what compulsory legislation prescribes. The law also imputes to a contract certain terms and conditions of employment if the contract itself is silent as to the points involved. This kind of "permissive" law allows expression of contrary intentions.

Individual labor law also includes a special class of legislation that is of a distinctly protective character. Some of these enactments aim to benefit all employees (limits on working hours, health and safety requirements), while others protect specific groups of employees (e.g., children, adolescents, women, mothers, and invalids). Breaches of these protective provisions will nearly always result in penalties, and labor protection law must accordingly be seen as a special branch of public law. Finally, the law of procedure, which serves for the enforcement of claims in the labor courts, is sometimes regarded as within the scope of individual labor law.

Collective labor law, on the other hand, concerns itself with the organizations of employers and employees, and with the problems of collective bargaining. It contains the legal provisions relating to the formation and jurisdiction of voluntary and statutory organizations, the establishment and functions of works councils *(Betriebsraete)* in factories, workshops, and other establishments, as well as provisions that regulate collective agreements and so-called workplace arrangements *(Betriebsvereinbarungen)*, and finally those rules that relate to strikes and lockouts.

Although legislation lays the foundation on which the edifice of industrial relations is built, legislation cannot in most instances provide more than a general framework in which specific arrangements must be designed to solve problems as they arise. Thus, supplementing legislation is a body of rules of a quasi-legislative character that stem from collective agreements, a network of rules that frequently interlock and overlap. The status and effectiveness of a particular rule depend upon the particular level in a closely constructed hierarchy at which it was made. The hierarchy of legal sources, in descending order of scope, is as follows:

> compulsory legislation (acts of Parliament and regulations)
> collective agreements
> workplace arrangements
> individual employment contracts
> permissive legislation
> work rules.

A rule enacted at a lower level has to be consistent with the higher level requirements that supercede it, in case of inconsistency. There is, however, one exception to this general rule, which has to do with the so-called doctrine of beneficialness. This doctrine is basic to Austrian labor law. According to the doctrine of beneficialness, a lower level rule is not considered inconsistent with a higher level rule if the former is more beneficial to the employee than the latter. Consequently, a lower level rule may in practice prevail over a higher level rule.

For example, on retirement, employee A seeks a pension from his employer. Legislation makes no provision for occupational pension schemes; but both the collective agreement and the particular workplace agreement applicable to A require the employer to pay a pension to retiring workers. Let us imagine that the collective agreement mandates a monthly pension of S1,000 (1,000 schillings) the workplace arrangement S1,400. When A was first hired, neither the collective nor the workplace arrangement then in force provided for a pension, but A's contract of employment contained a clause entitling A to a monthly retirement pension of S800. This clause was later superceded by both the workplace and the collective arrangements, since both were enacted at a level "superior" to A's employment contract. According to the doctrine of beneficialness, A is entitled to a pension of S1,400 a month, as laid down in the workplace arrangement, because he is better off under the terms of that arrangement.

The doctrine of beneficialness is, however, only applicable where conflicting rules were enacted at *different* levels. Where they arise at the *same* level, they are reconciled differently: the more recent enactment will, as a rule, be regarded as superceding the earlier. (There is only one exception: if the earlier enactment is clearly intended to cover the specific point at issue while the later one is more general, the specific enactment will prevail.) These so-called rules of abrogation also apply if two collective agreements or two workplace arrangements are incompatible with each other. A more recent collective agreement can reduce and even cancel a benefit introduced by an earlier one.

As a rule, the existence of an individual employment contract, whether written or oral, is an indispensable precondition for the application of labor law. Apart from establishing the initial relationship between employer and employee, individual contracts also regulate all questions left open by legislation and collective and workplace arrangements and confer specific benefits on particular employees.

Legal enactments have standardized many of the general conditions of work in Austria. The normal working week is forty hours; no more than ten hours may be worked in any one day; and overtime, paid at time and a half at least, can be worked only five hours in one week and sixty hours in any one year before requiring a special license. In addition to an annual holiday entitlement, employees are entitled to thirteen or if of a certain religious persuasion, fourteen paid feast days. White-collar workers are entitled to full sick pay for not less than six weeks in a year, and to half pay for four weeks thereafter; they must work for a full six months before becoming entitled to sick pay again. Blue-collar workers may, in similar circumstances, claim full pay for four weeks of sickness in a year; after a long period of employment they can claim full sick pay for a maximum of ten weeks in any one year. After sickness benefits have been exhausted, employees are eligible for cash payments under the sickness insurance scheme in which they are compulsorily enrolled. Employees who have to miss work to nurse a sick relative are entitled to full pay for a maximum of one working week a year.

In addition to regular pay, employees are entitled to two special bonuses a year, each equivalent to one month's pay, which are taxed at special rates favorable to the recipients. Terminated workers are entitled to severance pay unless they resign voluntarily or are summarily dismissed for gross misconduct; however, employees may resign after a minimum of ten years of service in order to claim retirement benefits under the social insurance scheme, and female employees who resign on the birth of a child retain their rights to severance pay. The amount of severance pay depends on seniority: after three years' employment, it equals one-sixth of annual wages, and after uninterrupted service of twenty-five years it equals one year's pay. If an employer becomes insolvent, his or her severance pay liability passes to a special fund to which all employers are required to contribute.

Dismissal without notice is permitted only for a reason, usually gross misconduct. In all other cases employees are entitled to a specified minimum notice, which must be given so that notice expires on one of the days in the year the law specifies for the purpose. As will be explained later, dismissed workers may have their dismissals reviewed. Employees are only fully liable for damages caused by their willful actions. In cases of employee negligence, the courts are empowered to reduce the extent of a worker's liability to an equitable level, and if negligence was only nominal, no liability at all is incurred.

In conclusion, a few words should be said on the matter of earnings. According to the most recent figures available from the Austrian Chambers of Labor Conference, in 1979 the weekly gross earnings of manual workers in manufacturing (excluding construction) were, for men, S2,673 and for women, S1,768. Piece-rate workers averaged S2,741 and S1,995, respectively. Net earnings amounted to approximately 77.0 percent of gross earnings. The average gross earnings of white-collar workers in industry amounted to S18,585 per month in 1979; because of their higher earnings and Austria's sharply progressive income tax structure, however, their net earnings amounted to only 73.5 percent of gross. On average, blue-collar workers worked 1,750 hours in 1979 and were paid for 2,059 hours. According to a survey carried out by the Vienna Chamber of Labor, in 1979 both blue- and white-collar workers spent 26.6 percent of their earnings on food, 9.8 percent on clothing, 9.0 percent on motor vehicles, 8.3 percent on housing, and 7.4 percent on furniture. Between 1975 and 1980 earnings went up by 41.9 percent, which corresponds to an annual average increase of 8.4 percent. During the same period prices for consumer goods went up by 5.9 percent a year.

CLASSIFICATION OF WORKERS: PRIVATE SECTOR

For historical reasons Austria's statutory labor law is split into a bewildering number of enactments. One characteristic feature of the law is that regulations that apply to employment in the private sector differ enormously from those that determine conditions of work in the public sector. In both sectors sharply distinct categories of workers can be identified.

In the private sector the distinction between blue- and white-collar workers is basic. Employees are assigned to one or the other class solely on the basis of the demands of their work. The law defines white-collar work quite flexibly, and classifies all other work as blue-collar.

Three classes of work carry white-collar status: commercial services, superior noncommercial services, and clerical services. Commercial services involve the typical work of merchants and business people, such as buying and selling, stock keeping, cash handling, accountancy, and customer service. The courts have recently been taking the view that superior noncommercial services require a certain level of responsibility and supervision of other employees, as well as a high degree of proficiency and expertise (which in turn presupposes previous training). Those who satisfy the standard include everyone from the manager of a business to the person in charge of a workshop or technical department, but the foreman or the person in charge of laborers is not included. Clerical services cover typical office work.

Some jobs have traditionally been classified as either white- or blue-collar positions, and the demarcation is accepted in such cases. Yet it is difficult to see why highly specialized craftspeople, whose work demands skill and experience and who are entrusted with substantial responsibility, should be denied white-collar status. Conversely, large groups of office workers continue to enjoy white-collar status even though new office technologies are lessening the demands their work makes on them. But attempts to produce a more sensible system of demarcation require group interests to enter the discussion—and that dooms attempts at reform because all groups of workers want white-collar status and will fight tooth and nail against their exclusion from the class. Rightly or wrongly, white-collar workers enjoy higher social prestige. Indeed, many blue-collar workers are even prepared to accept financial losses in exchange for the coveted white-collar status.

White-collar unions fiercely oppose the idea that the distinction between the two types of unions should be abolished. Abolition would, in fact, have far-reaching implications, for the organization of Austria's trade unions is based on the traditional distinction. White-collar workers at the factory level have their own representatives who are prepared to defend their independence. Moreover, the social security system also reflects the existence of two distinct classes of workers.

Legislators have abandoned the attempt to abolish the distinction or to change the criteria on which the distinction is based. Instead, legislation seeks to reduce the differences in terms and conditions of employment between the two classes, its final goal being equal rights for white- and blue-collar workers. Considerable progress has been made, and differences are now minimal (e.g., in periods of notice of termination and in reasons for dismissal without notice). But these legislative efforts have not been matched in the field of collective bargaining, for white- and blue-collar workers still tend to have different aims. Whether this divergence arises from different types of work or reflects a fundamental difference of worker attitudes is a moot point.

Why in practical terms does this basic distinction matter? The most striking evidence of its importance is pay. Collective agreements for blue-collar workers usually recognize only three groups of employees (apprentices, unskilled and semiskilled workers, and skilled craftspeople); wage rates are not linked to seniority; and pay is often tied to productivity. White-collar workers, on the other hand, have managed to establish in their collective agreements the principle that pay should be related to grades of work (e.g., in industry there are six such grades), and that in each grade pay should go up automatically every other year. Thus the earnings of white-collar workers, who tend to stay in the same job, will normally increase regularly, reaching a peak shortly before retirement, whereas the earnings of blue-collar workers only rise materially as long as their output grows, so that in their later years, as their productivity unavoidably declines, their earnings frequently decrease. This difference has great significance for old age pensions.

Within these two general classes of workers, the law does not uniformly regulate the terms and conditions of employment. Efforts to unify labor law and produce one single labor law code have been in progress since 1967, but the goal is still a long way off. For the time being, legislators content themselves with trying to achieve equal treatment piecemeal. The regulation of particular problems (e.g., civil liability and leave entitlement) is thus done in one statute applicable to white- and blue-collar workers alike. Other statutes, while upholding the continued validity of the various enactments relating to classes of employees, amend these separate pieces of legislation along identical lines. This partial codification is intended to pave the way for an all-embracing labor law code some time in the future.

Austrian law regarding employment conditions lacks coherence. In the private sector wages and salaries are on principle not fixed by statute. All other employment conditions of sufficient importance are regulated by special enactments that deal with specific categories of employees. The most important are the White-Collar Workers in Industry and Commerce Act of 1920, the White-Collar Workers in Agriculture and Forestry Act of 1923, the Journalists Act of 1920, the Theatrical Performers Act of 1922, and the Agricultural Laborers Act of 1948. On the other hand, the bulk of legislation relating to employment contracts deals only with the problems of specified groups of workers.

Yet the fragmentary nature of Austrian labor law is not as detrimental to the interests of employers and employees as one might think. Private publications provide up-to-date versions of applicable statutes, and collective agreements often quote verbatim the applicable legal provisions. The provisions of the relevant collective agreement are, as a rule, sufficient to deal with day-to-day problems.

In the field of collective labor law, partial codification has had some noteworthy successes. Collective agreements, workplace arrangements, works councils, and industrial democracy are all subject to uniform regulation in the Labor Relations Act *(Arbeitsverfassungsgesetz)* of 1973.

Classification of Workers: Public Sector

Before examining the situation in the public sector, we need to sketch the criteria that determine whether a certain activity of the state should be assigned to the public sector. The activities of the state (or any other public body such as a province or a municipality, since these entities are also juridical personalities) fall into two distinct categories. Some activities flow from constitutional powers—the state's duty to maintain law and order, for example—and such activities occur in the public sector. But the state also pursues purely commercial activities that do not involve its constitutional powers of coercion, and in recent years such commercial activities have increased both in volume and in importance. The state can integrate such activities into its administrative system, and in such cases both the undertaking and the people who run it belong to the public sector; or it may operate its enterprises as corporations under the terms of commercial law, in which case the companies concerned proceed in the same manner as privately owned corporations. Less fettered because they operate outside the state bureaucracy, their managers are responsible for the conduct of these enterprises only to the extent that directors of private companies are responsible to shareholders under company law. Such state-owned enterprises are regarded as operating in the private sector. They are compulsorily enrolled in the chambers of commerce system and sometimes even join voluntary entrepreneurs' associations. But their employees are still subject to private sector labor law.

Just as the distinction between white- and blue-collar workers is basic to the private sector, so the public sector distinguishes between established civil servants *(Beamte)* and nonestablished staff whose conditions of employment are determined by an employment contract. Established civil servants are employees of the state and stand in a special relationship to their employer based on public law. The relationship is not founded on contract and ostensibly arises from the state's unilateral power to appoint persons to posts in the civil service. Terms and conditions of service are not negotiable; they are determined by statute, and there is no room for individual bargaining, a fact of particular importance in the matter of pay.

The duties of the established civil service are categorized as "employment groups," and each civil servant belongs to a particular group according to his or her training or educational qualifications. A civil servant is assigned to one of nine service classes, depending on group and qualifications. Pay scales also take account of seniority. Thus pay in the civil service depends both on the kind of duties and on the length of service. Advancement happens on a timed basis; there is a pay raise every other year. But promotion to a more senior post is the only way in which the individual civil servant can progress in his or her career. Balancing these limitations, civil servants are in principle appointed for life. If they are absent from work on account of illness, they are entitled to full pay for an indefinite period of time; and retirement and invalid benefits are infinitely better than those for private sector employees. Because of these benefits, which often do not even depend on contributions by the employee, civil servants are only partially enrolled in the Austrian social security system.

Established civil servants were accorded these special conditions of service in order to secure them a large measure of independence and to strengthen them to resist outside pressures. Yet there are counterbalancing disadvantages: the rigidity inherent in the uniform regulation of conditions of service offers few incentives for efficiency.

When the state started to get involved in industry and commerce, it found the civil service inadequate for its needs. The government therefore began to employ persons who were expected to discharge duties of a commercial nature on the basis of individual employment contracts, as is customary in the private sector. The relationship between the state and "employees under contract" is governed by the provisions of private law; in other words, terms of employment for these individuals are subject to labor law and not to administrative law. A dispute between the state and an employee under contract falls within the jurisdiction of the labor courts, whereas an established civil servant must pursue his or her claim against the state through a formalistic administrative system. Employees under contract are fully enrolled in the social security system and are denied the privileges that civil servants enjoy. At the same time, their contracts are more flexible: they may receive a higher salary than civil servants in the same position.

The rapid expansion of the state's commercial activity has produced a steady increase in the numbers of employees under contract. In 1982 they numbered about 196,200, compared with 163,500 established civil servants. Civil servants as a rule perform those tasks that flow from the state's constitutional power to maintain law and order, while employees under contract run the state's commercial undertakings. The difference in the material conditions of employment of the two groups has been diminishing. Above all, the right of the state to terminate employees under contract has been drastically curtailed. Nowadays, the difference between the two has been reduced to two main points: civil servants enjoy the security of tenure, while employees under contract enjoy more flexible terms and conditions of service.

Both classes of state servants are, to all intents and purposes, outside collective bargaining. As a result, members of the civil service are keen to gain influence over legislation, since it is legislation that determines their conditions of service, and the public service unions have a particularly large membership. Although these trade unions cannot in a legal sense make collective agreements with the state, each new piece of legislation affecting public service is traditionally preceded by lengthy discussions between the government and the four unions. (In theory, the resultant compromises could be rejected by Parliament; however, because the government can be sure of a majority in Parliament, the danger does not in practice arise.) One further point also deserves to be noted: although minimum wages as fixed in a collective agreement are frequently exceeded in practice, no similar deviation from agreed pay scales is admissible insofar as established civil servants are concerned. Nevertheless, broadly speaking, pay in the civil service keeps pace with wages in the private sector.

The Collective Bargaining System

By the end of the nineteenth century, Austrian trade unions were attempting to fashion agreements about minimum working conditions with employers and the employers' organizations. These collective agreements steadily gained ground, and in 1920 Parliament gave them special legal effect. Since then, a finely meshed net of collective agreements has spread over the entire Austrian economy, and few workers in the private sector are not covered by a collective agreement of some kind. More recently, collective agreements have been supplemented by individual workplace arrangements.

Given the importance of extra legal agreements, statutes are of significance only in conferring minimum rights and benefits. These statutes actually provide a basic safety net, and trade unions frequently seek to ensure the continuation of newly won standards by having them incorporated into statutory labor law. Only in regard to wages and salaries have the social partners insisted on the right to negotiate agreements without the interference of lawmakers.

Very few empirical studies have examined the contents of collective agreements and workplace arrangements. Indeed, labor law specialists have confined themselves to scrutinizing legal regulations and related court judgments.

Collective Agreements

Under Austrian law a collective agreement is a contract in private law that is designed to regulate industrial relations. Collective agreements must be in writing and have to be registered with the appropriate authorities. The law directly confers the right to make collective agreements upon the statutory organizations (chambers) of employers and employees. Voluntary organizations that wish to become involved in the process of collective bargaining must apply for the right to become a party. Although this arrangement was devised to frustrate challenges to the validity of a collective agreement, it should be noted that in practice the Austrian Federation of Trade Unions (OGB) and other voluntary organizations (particularly on the employers' side) frequently apply for the right to conclude collective agreements, a right that is automatic when a voluntary organization satisfies criteria of size and scope. In this way the law excludes unrepresentative groups from collective bargaining, and in practical terms only the OGB and the chambers of commerce conclude collective agreements. (Trade unions, incidentally, are thus prevented from "picking off" employers one by one through individual negotiations.)

It is up to the contracting parties to determine the scope of a collective agreement. An agreement usually applies to a whole industry or group of similar industries and is valid throughout Austria; however, blue- and white-collar workers nearly always negotiate separate agreements. Those agreements made at the highest level—that is, when the OGB and the Federal Chamber of Commerce are the contracting parties—will apply to the entire work force of Austria. Such agreements are exceedingly rare, though they include the gradual reduction of the workweek from forty-eight to forty hours in 1959 and 1964 and the increase in annual minimum vacation entitlements to three weeks in 1964.

A collective agreement affects all wage earners employed in the branch of industry or commerce that the agreement covers, regardless of their duties (usually subject to the proviso that white- and blue-collar workers negotiate separate agreements). It will frequently be supplemented by special agreements that regulate particular problems or deal with the employment conditions of smaller groups of workers. This practice affords a maximum of flexibility in framing employment conditions, and the freedom that the contracting parties enjoy in this respect tends to strengthen the position of the top management of the organizations concluding the agreement.

Collective agreements contain two distinct kinds of provisions. The first creates rights and obligations only between the signatories, for example, how the agreement should be terminated and what kind of arbitration should be used in the case of a dispute. This sort of provision has effects identical to those inherent in any private contract.

The second kind of provision is normative in that it is binding on third parties who did not participate in the making of the agreement. Austrian law makes normative provisions in a collective agreement binding upon all employers and employees within the scope of the agreement, even if they did not want the provisions and even if they received no notice of them. Thus a collective agreement has the force of law: it has an immediate and compulsory effect on everyone involved. Nevertheless, the principle of beneficialness (see chapter 2) also applies here, for a provision in a workplace arrangement or an individual employment contract will prevail over the terms of a collective agreement if it is more beneficial to the employee. Claims stemming from collective agreements can be enforced by court action, and such rights cannot be restricted or rescinded.

The parties to a collective agreement cannot, of course, regulate any question they please by means of a normative provision. On the contrary, law limits the subjects that can be dealt with in this manner to questions that regularly appear in individual employment contracts, such as job description, rates of pay, leave entitlement, and sick pay. Normative provisions cannot limit an employer's right to hire whomever he or she wishes (that is, they cannot be used to impose a closed shop). Similarly, workers cannot be required to set aside part of their pay for dues. Some uncertainties attend these limits; for example, it was long unclear whether the rights of works councils to participate in the management of business could, by means of a collective agreement, be extended beyond the limits defined by legislation. Parliament eventually restricted the function of collective agreements to implementing the statutory rules about codetermination.

Collective agreements currently may also provide for the setting up of institutions (e.g., training centers, benevolent funds, pension endowments) to be owned and managed jointly by the contracting organizations, and for the establishment of direct contractual relations, involving defined rights and duties, between those institutions and the individual employers and employees. Moreover, collective agreements may make valid exceptions to statutory prohibitions (particularly those relating to maximum hours of work) and fill in the gaps deliberately left in new legislation by introducing more detail (e.g., regarding the way sick pay is to be calculated). These concessions, and others like them, recognize that legislation is framed at too general a level to allow its indiscriminate application to the whole of the Austrian economy. The parties to a collective agreement are assumed to know their particular branch of industry or commerce and are assumed competent to decide on exemptions from statute requirements or greater detail in regulations. As the negotiating strength of the two parties is roughly equal, the law is not vulnerable to the possibility that the working class will lose necessary protection. Moreover, the right to waive rules gives union negotiators a bargaining chip to be cashed in for concessions on other matters.

An individual employee does not have to be or ever have been a member of the union to be affected by collective agreements. Individual conditions of employment are determined by collective agreement if the employer is a member of the employers' organization that concluded the agreement. For example, a collective agreement for blue-collar workers in the electrical industry covers all workers in a given electrical engineering company (provided its owner is a member of the contracting employers' organization), regardless of their duties or the fact that the company is entirely nonunion. This is known as the "outsider effect." At first glance it may seem strange that a trade union should be entitled to conclude agreements that bind employees who do not belong to the union and who cannot be regarded as having authorized the union to act on their behalf. But a collective agreement confined to union members would be by Austrian standards intolerable, for it would result in different conditions and terms of employment for union and nonunion workers in the same establishment.

As most collective agreements on the employers' side are concluded by the chambers of commerce, in which employers are required to be members, this outsider effect results in collective agreements applying to all the white-collar or all the blue-collar workers in a particular branch. The OGB has never voiced objections about the outsider effect, and it has made no attempt to enforce a closed shop system (which would have run afoul of Austrian law anyway). Its membership is so large that the federation is resigned to free riders, who do not contribute toward its operating costs. Nor has the OGB made any serious attempt to levy a "solidarity contribution" from nonmembers or to obtain preferential treatment for union members in collective agreements. (Such attempts would in all probability be ruled illegal, although no court has yet had to rule on them.) Thus the outsider effect has stood the test of time; there are at least no visible signs of tension between members and nonmembers of the trade union movement, while the outsider effect validates the federation's claim to speak on behalf of all Austrian workers.

Collective agreements are usually indefinite in duration, and they are terminable by notice on either side. Only wage arrangements are valid for a finite time, usually twelve or fifteen months.

No organization can be forced to conclude a collective agreement or even to enter negotiations. Similarly, the law provides no facilities for mediation when negotiations fail. When negotiations do break down, however, leaders of the respective partnership organizations will customarily step in as mediators, and, if the matter is of sufficient importance, the government will also become involved. Grave conflicts are, however, very rare. Industrial action remains a last resort, strikes are seldom called, and lockouts are virtually unknown. In practice, the collective bargaining system works smoothly.

Collective agreements fulfill several functions. First and foremost they provide protection for the labor force; they lay down minimum standards in rights and benefits and limit the amount of work an employee is required to perform, providing an effective barrier against exploitation. Once the negotiated terms of employment are set down in a collective agreement, they are, at least for a time, fixed beyond cavil, and the social conflicts that sparked negotiations originally are resolved. Hence collective agreements are peace-making instruments, and this function is of the greatest significance. Moreover, collective agreements continually develop and expand existing labor laws, thus paving the way for new legislation.

It is also worth noting that collective agreements make an important contribution toward unifying working conditions in the specific branches of industry or commerce that they cover. With a view to increasing this effect, the parties to collective agreements have adopted new wage policies in the last few years. By inserting "effective wage clauses" in their agreements, they seek to reduce wage drift—the gap between minimum rates laid down in collective agreements and the usually much higher rates actually paid. For example, a collective agreement may increase minimum wage rates by 10 percent and provide at the same time that actual wages increase by 6 percent. This tactic ensures some benefit for every worker, while employers are often obliged to increase the total wage pool by only 6 percent. Pool arrangements enable employers to use an overall 6 percent increase to reward individual efficiency or productivity at a higher rate.

The labor courts hold exclusive jurisdiction over the interpretation of the provisions of a collective agreement, and how they exercise their prerogative is similar to how they interpret a statute or statutory regulation. The wording of the agreement is in such cases paramount; the courts try to identify the intentions of the contracting parties as expressed in the text of the agreement, but they have consistently refused to question negotiators about intended meanings. The reason for this refusal is clear. Being binding on third parties, collective agreements may in principle be interpreted only in the light of their texts. If contracting parties are dissatisfied with a court's interpretation, they are free to amend the clause or clauses concerned, even retroactively, if need be.

When the signatory on the employers' side is a voluntary organization, any previous agreement negotiated by a statutory organization that covers the same ground lapses, as far as the members of the voluntary organization and their workers are concerned. Such situations are unlikely to arise, but when they do, the collective agreement covers only the members of the voluntary organization. Such a state of affairs may make those employers who are not tied to the provisions of the collective agreement more competitive, of course, which might in turn undermine the agreement. To avoid this problem, trade unions can request the appropriate authorities to extend the collective agreement in question to employees outside its original scope. If the request is granted, the collective agreement attains the status of a quasi-statutory instrument *(Satzung)*, which is applicable to all affected workers who were formerly excluded from the agreement. Before a collective agreement may be made a quasi-statutory instrument, however, it must usually pertain to more than half the employees in the particular branch of industry or commerce involved.

Few areas of employment lack employers' organizations that could get involved in collective bargaining (one example is domestic services). In these areas, there can be no collective agreement and consequently no quasi-statutory instruments. Authorities are thus empowered to fix minimum wages on the motion of the trade union concerned, though they cannot concern themselves with any other condition of employment. Quasi-statutory instruments and minimum wage rates lapse as soon as a "normal" collective agreement covering the relevant segment of employment has entered into effect.

Thus under Austrian law the voluntary organizations on both sides of industry are primarily responsible for regulating terms and conditions of employment, through collective agreements; statutory organizations are of only secondary importance; and the public authorities are last in line. Indeed, public authorities can only extend the scope of an existing collective agreement, without having any say as to its contents, and fix minimum wages where no employers' organization exists. The rights of the state are subsidiary to those of the social partners, and the rights of the statutory organizations are subsidiary to those of the voluntary organizations.

Workplace Arrangements

If the staff of a particular industrial or commercial establishment elects a works council, the council can enter into written contracts with management *(Betriebsvereinbarungen)*; the effects of these "workplace arrangements" are analogous to those of collective agreements. There are many such arrangements in Austria, and they effectively prevent employers from determining work conditions unilaterally. The normative clauses in workplace arrangements, like similar clauses in collective agreements, automatically apply in each individual employment contract and will override any contrary contractual clause (subject to the doctrine of beneficialness). Workplace arrangements are, however, limited by law. In addition to certain matters to be considered in detail below, legislation specifies that workplace arrangements may address profit-sharing schemes, occupational pension arrangements, work safety measures, and the manner in which a works council can cooperate with management in matters of training facilities, welfare arrangements, and temporary extensions or reductions of the workday. The law, however, excludes wages (hourly rates or monthly salaries, as well as allowances and bonuses) from workplace arrangements. These questions are the exclusive province of collective agreements, if they are to be settled by collective bargaining at all, though the parties to a collective agreement may delegate the responsibility of bargaining for wage or salary levels to works councils. Workplace arrangements affect all blue- or white-collar workers, as the case may be, employed in the workplace concerned. Claims arising from these arrangements can be enforced in the labor courts.

Employers need the consent of their works councils before they can introduce measures in four general areas—discipline, staff questionnaires, control measures, and piecework rates. Conversely, a works council cannot force the employer to adopt specific measures in these four areas. Other matters are subject to the give and take of true bargaining without limitations, such as when shifts start and stop and how wages are to be paid. If no agreement on these matters is reached, either party can refer the matter at issue to an ad hoc arbitration board, whose decision has the effect of a workplace arrangement and is binding upon both parties. All other workplace arrangements are, however, voluntary, and an uncooperative party cannot be forced to conclude arrangements it does not favor. Arrangements may be of either definite or indefinite duration. Indefinite arrangements are liable to termination by notice from either side, but their effects will extend beyond the termination date until a new arrangement is made. Once such an arrangement has expired, newly engaged workers are not affected by the arrangement, and the employer becomes able to contract out of the arrangement with each worker. Arrangements of definite duration expire on the appointed date without aftereffects. On this latter point, of course, workplace arrangements differ from collective agreements, whose normative clauses continue to be applicable after the agreement has ended, irrespective of how it was terminated. As workplace arrangements of definite duration have no aftereffects, they offer an opportunity for time-limited social experiments.

The orderliness for which the law aims is not always to be found in practice. Employers and works councils often do not know the statutory limits on workplace arrangements, and even when they do, they sometimes deliberately flout them. Thus, for example, almost all works councils seek to obtain pay raises for their constituents at the plant level. Most larger enterprises have wage scales that were introduced or amended through workplace arrangements, in defiance of the law. The employer and works council usually abide by the terms they have agreed to rather than question their legal validity. Indeed, in recent years the courts have recognized these arrangements, although they hold them to be unenforceable. (The courts argue that where such an arrangement operates, its terms are implied in every individual employment contract between employer and employee.)

The legal effects of these arrangements differ from those of admissible (normative) workplace arrangements, especially when one side, usually the employer, wants to renege on or amend the agreement. This has proved to be a serious problem in times of economic crisis. For example, if a workplace arrangement provides for the payment of an occupational pension and the employer's financial position subsequently makes it impossible to discharge pension obligations in full, the employer may terminate the arrangement by giving due notice to the works council. Such notice excludes new employees from the pension scheme, though it does not affect those already on the payroll. The works council, perhaps in exchange for some other concession, may even agree to a fresh workplace arrangement, thus permitting a temporary or a permanent reduction in the employer's pension payments. As a new workplace arrangement ends the aftereffects of the prior arrangement, the reduction of the pension immediately and directly affects all employees, even those already receiving a pension. Thus a firm may be kept going, jobs may be saved, and last but not least the continued payment of pensions, albeit at a reduced rate, may be secured.

By way of comparison, take the case of an inadmissible workplace arrangement that provides for a 10 percent wage increase. (The law, it will be recalled, only recognizes such an arrangement by holding that it is implied in every individual employment contract.) If after an economic setback the employer, to save the business and its jobs, subsequently wants to reduce wages to their former level, and even if the works council were to agree to the wage cut in a new workplace arrangement, the works council concession would have no legal effect. The employer would still have to obtain the consent of every single employee, for according to the doctrine of beneficialness, claims that rest on individual employment contracts cannot be denied or reduced by a workplace arrangement, even by an arrangement that the law recognizes as admissible.

WORKERS' PARTICIPATION IN MANAGEMENT

At the end of World War I, Parliament recognized, at least in principle, the right of the working class to have a say in the running of their employers' businesses. This right remained embryonic until after 1945.

Austria approaches the matter of power sharing between workers and management (codetermination) from two different angles. First, the law requires that works councils should be elected in all industrial or commercial establishments that employ at least five people, and that these works councils should represent the interests of their fellow workers vis-à-vis management. Second, workers in any public limited company are represented on its policy-making boards, in a sense acting the part of entrepreneurs. In this way employees' representatives are absorbed within the company's policy-making machinery while remaining opposite of management in collective bargaining. Where no works council exists, there can be no codetermination. The election of works councils is therefore of paramount importance for the system to work.

The Austrian system of codetermination is in essence two-tiered, involving a sharp division of functions between works councils, on the one hand, and trade unions and the chambers of labor, on the other. At the plant level, workers are represented by works councils; in general matters such as economic policy, wage policy, taxation, and social security, workers participate in the policy-making process through the unions and the chambers of labor, within the framework of the social partnership. Accordingly, it is necessary to distinguish carefully between codetermination at the factory level and codetermination at the industrial or national level.

Works councils are theoretically independent; they can decide whether to seek advice from unions and chambers, and they are under no legal obligation to consult. In practice, however, there are close ties among the organizations. Most of the members of works councils are union members, though those who elect them need not be. Candidates for a works council are nominated by their fellow employees, not by the trade unions, though the unions usually manage to get nominees whom they favor. Indeed, members of works councils, particularly in larger establishments, are often senior officials in the trade union movement, so they both influence union policies and are influenced by them. Nevertheless, members of a works council have to take account primarily of the needs and interests of their constituents.

Austrian works councils are composed exclusively of employees' representatives (a feature that distinguishes them from the joint works councils of other European countries, on most of which management is represented). Senior managerial staff are not considered employees insofar as works councils and codetermination are concerned. Thus managing directors and factory managers are excluded, but not heads of department.

The period of office on a works council is three years. Members are elected by all employees of the establishment who are at least eighteen years of age, in a secret ballot and according to the principle of proportional representation. Blue- and white-collar workers are usually represented by different works councils. The number of members on a particular council depends on the number of employees in the establishment in question.

Number of employees	*Number of members on works council*
5–9	1
10–19	2
20–50	3
51–100	4
100–1,000	1 further member/every 100 members
1,000 plus	1 further member/every 400 members

Members must be Austrian citizens and must be employed in the same establishment as their electors. Each unit that is independent and that has a separate organization constitutes an establishment *(Betrieb)*, which is to say a bargaining unit, within the meaning of the law.

In the case of small businesses, "establishments" and "enterprise" coincide. In the case of large businesses, each single factory (and occasionally also its various branches) is a separate establishment. A place of work is treated as an establishment only if all major decisions affecting its current business are made on site and the work performed there is not merely subordinate in character to the work of the enterprise at large. Thus the principal workshop and the head office of a business in the electrical industry are establishments. But workshops, even if far from headquarters, where assembly work not involving the manufacture of end products is undertaken under the guidance of a foreman and in strict compliance with instruction from headquarters, do not constitute establishments. Nevertheless, a department of the same business that constructs high-voltage power installations for the company's customers and that enjoys a large measure of independence in technical matters does constitute a separate establishment. Where an enterprise consists of more than one establishment, the elected members of the several works councils will elect from among their own numbers a central works council, to concern itself with problems that affect the enterprise as a whole. It should be noted that the concept of what constitues an establishment is of the greatest importance, for there is no employee representation below that level. The manual laborers in a workshop or the white-collar workers in an office cannot elect their own works councils.

Members of works councils are not delegates—that is, in the performance of their functions they are in no way forced to follow instructions from their constituents. Although theoretically, workers can demand a special staff meeting where a two-thirds' majority can remove all the members of the works council from office, in fact, this happens very rarely. Some works councils take advantage of the discretion conferred upon them; others always discuss important matters at staff meetings. Staff meetings may also levy special contributions from all employees of the enterprise to meet those costs of the works council not borne by the employer. Works council funds, as these special levies are called, exist mainly in larger enterprises and may also be used to finance social schemes that benefit the staff.

Employers are required to give time off with full pay for members to attend works council meetings, and in larger establishments one or several members of the works council are relieved of all work-related duties to concentrate full time on council business. Each member of the works council is, moreover, entitled to two weeks' special leave at the employer's expense to attend council-related courses. As members of works councils are more likely to incur their employers' displeasure, the law forbids discrimination against them because of their office. Above all, they cannot be fired unless the appropriate state authority gives its consent, and consent may be given only for certain statutorily defined reasons.

This privileged position also carries a number of drawbacks. Works councils seldom change personnel; a person once elected is likely to remain on the council for several terms of office. Members thus risk becoming bureaucratic functionaries and losing touch with job-related skills. Such a loss of expertise will militate against a person's prospects for advancement and promotion. Many members of works councils thus seek careers in the trade union movement or in a political party. Some chairs of works councils in larger establishments have even succeeded in getting elected to Parliament. Although the risk of works council members becoming estranged from their rank and file is inherent in the system, there is no movement to introduce a rota system for council membership.

Members of works councils regard themselves as representatives of the entire staff as well as of each individual employee vis-à-vis the employer. They often informally mediate conflicts within their establishments, more often than not easing tensions and preventing formal labor strife. Over and above the role of peacemaker, works council members are entitled to certain rights regarding codetermination. These rights range from being kept up to date by the employer about the economic situation of the business and being consulted about various decisions, to supervising conformity with particular legal requirements in the plant and becoming directly involved in the making of business decisions.

In codetermination the powers of the works council sometimes resemble those of minority shareholders in a company: a works council has no legal means of compelling an employer to take or refrain from taking a given measure. In other matters the works council is entitled to contest an employer's decision before the state authorities. In some instances the works council can even force its will upon an unwilling employer (through "compulsory" workplace arrangements). Finally, the employer may only take some measures of a more general character with the concurrence of the works council, whose consent cannot be replaced by the ruling or decision of any state authority.

In general matters, the works council helps improve the flow of information between management and staff. Members are entitled to all information necessary for the proper discharge of the council's functions; at the quarterly conferences held between the employer and the works council, the employer must inform the council of all current events and problems of major importance. The works council can intervene on any matter in which the staff takes a legitimate interest, and the employer is bound at least to listen. The works council is authorized to satisfy itself that its enterprise is in compliance with all legal enactments made for the benefit of the working population. In particular, it is empowered to scrutinize pay accounts, inspect personnel files (with the consent of the employees concerned), and superintend the employer's observation of social insurance laws and work safety regulations.

In regard to the specific tasks of works councils, the Industrial Relations Act distinguishes three areas of codetermination: the works council's right to be involved in all decisions affecting the careers of individual members of staff (codetermination in staff management); its right to a say in the settlement of problems affecting all or most of the staff (codetermination in social affairs); and finally, its right to concern itself with decisions affecting the economic situation of the enterprise (codetermination in economic affairs).

The extent of codetermination in staff management varies. Employers must discuss the proposed engagement of new staff, promotions, and the allocation of firm-owned housing with the works council, though council consent is not mandatory. Permanent transfer of an employee to an inferior post, however, requires the consent of the works council or, if that consent is withheld, the approval of a specialized state authority, the Conciliation Department. If the department also refuses approval, the attempt to transfer the employee in question must be abandoned. Disciplinary penalties may be imposed only with the consent of the council.

Employers wishing to terminate, by notice, the employment contract of a worker must, before giving notice, inform the works council of their intentions. If the works council agrees, notice can be given and the employee has no recourse. If, despite objection by the works council, the employer persists in serving notice of termination, the council can have the validity of the termination reviewed by the Conciliation Department. If it finds cause, the department can declare the notice of termination null and void.

There are only two grounds on which the propriety of a notice of dismissal can be successfully challenged. The first is to allege that the employer's true motive for firing the worker is illegal, for example, because the worker has joined a trade union. The second is of greater importance: to allege that the employer has failed to pay sufficient regard to the social implications of dismissal. In this case, evidence must be submitted showing that the worker concerned would be particularly hard hit by the loss of the job, for example because chances of alternative employment are poor, family commitments are onerous, or because dismissal would require the worker to take an inferior job elsewhere. The Conciliation Department may nevertheless uphold the dismissal if the employer can justify it on the grounds of the worker's conduct or propensities (e.g., shoddy work or a quarrelsome disposition) or by reason of the need to reduce the work force (e.g., in connection with rationalization or a planned reduction in output). The Conciliation Department cannot concern itself as to whether a reduction in the number of workers is really necessary for efficiency reasons. Instead, it must decide whether another employee, to be named by the works council, would be less adversely affected by the loss of his or her job. In this manner the Conciliation Department compares the social impact of dismissal upon two different employees (the so-called social comparison). If the works council does not challenge the dismissal, or if no works council exists, the individual worker can directly contest the notice, but in such cases the Conciliation Department is not empowered to make social comparisons.

Thus Austrian law generally prefers to entrust the protection of workers' individual interests to the works council. If the council consents to a transfer, a dismissal, or a disciplinary penalty, there is nothing the affected worker can do about it. In such cases the works council represents not one single employee but the entire staff. Thus in those rare cases where the interests of the individual clash with those of the majority, the individual derives no benefit from codetermination—a situation apparently inherent in any system of collective protection.

In the matter of dismissals the works council aims to strike a reasonable balance between efficiency and social implications. If employer and works council agree that dismissals are unavoidable, it is at least desirable that outsiders with little knowledge of the facts of the case be excluded from passing judgment. On the whole, the concept has proved its worth. The danger that the system might be used to fire members of an unpopular minority without good cause, by concerted action on the part of the employer and the works council, is admittedly present. It has provoked much adverse criticism from labor law scholars. However, the social partners are interested, for different reasons, in maintaining the current system.

In social affairs, workplace arrangements are the proper arena in which works councils exercise their rights to codetermination. The existence of a workplace arrangement implies that employer and works council have agreed upon conditions of employment rather than the employer determining them unilaterally or by bargaining with each individual employee. Employers, it will be recalled, are in many areas at liberty to subscribe to or to reject a workplace arrangement proposed by the works council; in some instances the arbitration board may compel employers to accept a works council's recommendation, and in the four areas specified earlier the employer cannot proceed with a proposed measure in the absence of works council agreement.

The involvement of the works council with the economic affairs of the enterprise generates the most controversial issues within codetermination. First and foremost is the right of the works council to be informed and consulted. Employers are bound to keep the works council informed of the economic situation of the enterprise and (unless the business is truly small) to submit copies of the balance sheet automatically to the council. The works council also has a right to be consulted before the employer takes certain defined steps. Employers are entitled unilaterally to effect major alterations in the organization and structure of the business (e.g., by adopting rationalization measures, by changing the purpose of the business, by replacing existing plant with new machinery, or by closing workshops), but only after discussions with the works council. If the proposed changes threaten the staff with severe losses, works councils can suggest a "social plan," consisting of measures that would eliminate or minimize the effects of the proposed changes.

The social plan may include retraining, compensation payments, and similar measures. If the employer refuses to agree, the works council can refer its social plan to an arbitration board, which may order the employer to adopt the suggested measures, thus incorporating them in a compulsory workplace arrangement. In the largest enterprises, the works council may lodge a formal protest against any far-reaching economic decision the management has taken or proposes. Such a protest will ultimately come before an economic commission of the state on which the social partners are equally represented. But the commission can do no more than express a nonbinding opinion on the case, and anyway it is customary for representatives of the partnership organizations, and also usually of the federal and provincial government, to embark on informal consultations in serious cases.

The central feature of the Austrian system of codetermination in the sphere of economic affairs is a requirement that one-third of the members of the supervisory boards of public limited companies (*Aktiengesellschaften*) should be employees' representatives. To appreciate the impact of this requirement, it is necessary to know that public limited companies use a three-tier system of policy making and management. Shareholders form an assembly to elect representatives to the company's supervisory board. This board, in turn, appoints the members of the board of directors, and no decision of major importance may be taken by the latter without the express approval of the former.

Employees' representatives are, therefore, directly involved both in overseeing the work of the board of directors and its individual members and in the policy-making process of the company. Special resolutions to appoint and remove members of the board of directors and the chair and deputy chair of the supervisory board must be endorsed by a majority of members of the supervisory board *and* by a majority of the shareholders' representatives on that board. This requirement of a "double majority" is intended to prevent employees' representatives from combining with minority shareholders to determine the composition of the board of directors against the wishes of the shareholder majority. These rules are of particular importance in nationalized companies, where membership on supervisory boards is proportional to the political parties' strength in Parliament and where members of the supervisory boards are party nominees.

The right of workers to have their own representatives on the supervisory boards of public limited companies has been extended to other legal entities, such as private limited companies (*Gesellschaften mit beschraenkter Haftung*), cooperative societies, and mutual assurance associations. In such organizations, however, the right is of less practical significance as their supervisory boards are less important. No similar rights of codetermination exist in the cases of sole traders and partnerships. Moreover, codetermination in economic affairs is restricted to commercial undertakings. Nonprofit and advocacy organizations in politics, religion, charity, science, and other such fields ("tendency establishments," as they are known) are exempted from codetermination because of the fear that the system might distort or interfere with the very aims these undertakings seek to propagate. The media are entitled to similar, though more limited, protection of their "tendencies." In fact the staff of the state-owned Broadcasting and Television Corporation has a disproportionately high level of representation at the various levels of the corporation's management.

In sum, the practical importance of the works council system varies from firm to firm. Although there are no reliable empirical studies, it is common knowledge that some works councils fail to make full use of their powers, while others have managed to extend their powers to fields not covered by law. (The latter observation applies with particular force to the nationalized sector, where works councils have enormous influence, particularly in staff management and personnel policy.) On the whole, the system of codetermination works smoothly. Its principal merits are an improved flow of information between management and workers and a higher consciousness of the social aspects of work. On the other hand, the system carries the risk of delaying necessary and sometimes urgent reactions to changes in the economic situation. But it is nevertheless incontrovertible that the system as practiced at all levels has contributed greatly to the avoidance of industrial warfare in Austria.

STRIKES AND LOCKOUTS

Because Austria has devised effective methods for settling social conflicts, strikes and lockouts are very rare. The mere threat of serious industrial action triggers numerous informal mechanisms, all designed to nip the conflict in the bud. Figures on strikes and lockouts illustrate the situation—and it must not be forgotten that since 1975 the Austrian economy has shivered before the cold wind of recession as much as other industrial countries.

In 1980, to provide some recent background, there were nationwide strikes of brewery workers, which lasted fourteen hours, and the office staff of insurance companies, which lasted five hours, as well as seven other minor strikes. In 1981 there was only one strike in all of industry, a token strike of the employees in distributive trades.

At the time of the monarchy and under the First Republic, by comparison, Austria's labor relations were not essentially different from those in other European countries. Thus it was only after World War II that Austria began to diverge from other European countries. This de-

TABLE 3.1

Strikes in Austria, 1951–81

Year	Strike Hours	Number of Strikers	Average Length of Strikes (hours/minutes)
1951	677,452	31,555	21/28
1956	1,227,292	43,249	28/23
1961	911,025	38,338	23/46
1966	570,846	120,922	4/43
1971	29,614	2,431	12/11
1975	44,098	3,783	11/39
1976	4,711	2,352	2/00
1977	86	43	2/00
1978	81,788	699	117/00
1979	6,111	786	7/46
1980	135,684	24,181	5/37
1981	32,188	17,115	1/52
1982	2,755	91	30/16

Source: *Arbeit und Wirtschaft* 5(1983):7.

velopment is the visible effect of the Austrian system of social partnership.

On the rare occasions that industrial conflict has broken out, peace has been restored eventually by economic rather than legal means. After the battle has raged for a (usually very short) time, the conflicting par-

TABLE 3.2

Strikes and Lockouts in Austria, 1920–32

Year	Number of Incidents	Workers Affected	Working Days Lost
Strikes			
1920	329	179,352	927,402
1924	401	268,696	2,295,493
1928	242	32,948	562,992
1932	30	5,429	79,942
Lockouts			
1920	6	5,718	93,398
1924	46	28,182	520,616
1928	24	5,342	95,032
1932	3	1,217	110,221

Source: Theodor Tomandl, *Streik und Aussperrung als Mittel des Arbeitskampfes* (Vienna: Springer, 1965), p. 34.

ties come to terms with each other and in the process also settle controversies that arose while the fight was on. Hence the courts have handed down only a very few high-level rulings, for they have seldom been concerned with cases of industrial warfare. Criminal offenses (mostly involving property damage and bodily injury) perpetrated in the course of industrial disputes become the subject of criminal proceedings very infrequently—for the simple reason that the culprits usually cannot be identified.

The authorities attempt to maintain a policy of strict neutrality in industrial conflicts. By and large, the police interfere only in pressing emergencies. Since the repeal in 1870 of provisions making strikes and lockouts criminal offenses, only a few marginally important questions have been regulated by statute. To quote a few examples: employment offices cannot direct job seekers to undertakings whose work force is on strike; an agreement binding the parties to engage in industrial conflict or to support other persons so engaged has no legal effect; striking workers are not eligible for unemployment benefits; preventing persons willing to work from doing so constitutes a punishable offense. A statute of 1914 forbids civil servants from striking, but the statute has not been invoked for decades, and civil servants who have downed tools have been subject neither to criminal proceedings nor to disciplinary action. Strike action within the civil service is, therefore, tolerated.

The Austrian Constitution ignores industrial conflict altogether, so there is no constitutionally guaranteed right to strike. Industrial action is generally tolerated as long as it does not conflict with the general law of the land. This attitude tacitly acknowledges industrial action as legitimate, but it is distinct from a specific right to strike. (Only in the latter case would a worker joining an official strike not be in breach of his or her employment contract.) As a corollary, the tacit rather than the specific right results in strikes and lockouts being treated on the same legal footing. For the sake of simplicity, we deal only with strikes, mainly because lockouts are so rare. The reader should remember that what is said of strikes also applies to lockouts. Moreover, in the absence of specific legal provisions, academic research has worked out the basic rules regarding both strikes and lockouts. What follows expounds only those concepts on which a general consensus of opinion exists.

Strike organizers commit a punishable offense only if they transgress the provisions of criminal law—for example, by using violence. In principle, strike organizers incur no civil liability with respect to an employer's financial losses except where the strike is directed against a third party (e.g., the government). Similarly, strikes to enforce a legal right are unlawful, since enforcement of legal rights falls within the exclusive jurisdiction of the courts.

In regard to striking, the parties to a collective agreement have a special duty: during the currency of the agreement, the parties must refrain from any industrial action, or from lending support to such action, if the dispute relates to a point settled in the collective agreement. (Thus this obligation is only relative: it does not extend to strikes over working conditions not regulated in the agreement, or to strikes after the agreement has expired.) But in practice, the trade unions have called several strikes without having terminated the collective agreement in question by due notice. Had they been sued for damages by the employers, judgment would probably have gone against them, but no such suit has yet been brought.

Strike organizers are obliged to take all reasonable steps to prevent outrages in the course of the strike. Following a strike of Viennese manual laborers in the distributive trades in 1961, suit was brought against the OGB for damages. Some workers, all of them union members, had prevented twelve wagons of bananas from being unloaded, and the fruit went bad. In this widely followed "banana case," the Supreme Court of Judicature dismissed the plaintiff's claim on the grounds that the federation was not responsible for the event that occasioned the damage. Though the judgment aroused severe criticism, there has been no further legal ruling on the question.

How does Austrian law deal with an individual employee or employer who does no more than take part in a strike or a lockout? An employee who goes on strike stops work without terminating his or her employment contract and thus acts in breach of contract. The same applies to employers who lock out workers and stop paying wages. A breach of contract by one party entitles the other party to terminate the contract without notice and to claim damages for losses sustained. Thus if workers go out on strike, the employer is entitled to fire them on the spot. The workers could lose their jobs and forfeit financial claims against the employer. Moreover, the employer can claim damages for any loss.

It is notable that the Austrian trade unions resign themselves to these consequences. Their acquiescence is based on several reasons. After all, the legal position applies in equal measure to employers and lockouts.

Each worker affected by a lockout can terminate his or her employment contract and claim damages from the employer. Such a claim will as a rule be capable of satisfaction, since the employer's property assets will, in most cases, suffice to satisfy the workers' claims; in the reverse case, however, an employer's claim will remain a dead letter for lack of funds on the part of the defendant. In practice, the risk of workers losing their jobs should not be exaggerated, for the employer will continue to need staff in the future. In these circumstances an employer will exercise the right to dismiss striking workers only if the employer knows that replacements are available or that the striker's job can be abolished altogether. Therefore only a tiny minority of strikers are really exposed to the danger of dismissal. Indeed, leading trade unionists have suggested that the danger of losing one's job might conceivably even be a salutary brake on frivolous and capricious strikes.

The unions are growing less and less ambitious about bringing all workers in a single establishment or a specific branch of the economy out on strike. Modern strike strategy, rather, aims to paralyze the greatest number of establishments with the smallest number of strikers. Therefore, only workers in key positions or particularly important supply operations strike. This practice keeps the number of strikers, and hence the amount of strike pay, low without lessening the economic impact on employers. Workers who are put out of work though willing to perform their duties will insist on their wages being paid even though there is no work available for them. Employers more often than not do go on paying wages in such a situation, though the courts have not ruled on their obligation to do so. A change in the law, recognizing cessation of work in a strike as lawful and suspending employment contracts, would produce a similar effect on the legality and consequences of a lockout, which would then also suspend the employment contracts concerned. Employers could then react to partial strikes by locking out employees for whom there is no work, a device that employers in the Federal Republic of Germany have been able to use since 1955. A change in the legal status of strikes would, because of its repercussions on lockouts, stop the unions from employing their current strike tactics, and thus the current union attitude toward existing strike law is a rational one.

Offenses by individuals cannot be excused on the grounds that they were committed during a strike or lockout. Criminal liability and civil liability for damages stemming from assault and willful or negligent damage to property are not diminished by the fact that an individual acted in connection with industrial action. In other words, the general law of crime and tort applies, even if cases are difficult to prove in practice. There are also several offenses specific to industrial conflict (e.g., coercion by threats of force of persons willing to work). Picketing, on the other hand, is admissible, as long as peaceful means are used to persuade workers to join the strike.

Legal Protection and Enforcement of Claims

Special courts, namely the labor courts, have jurisdiction over disputes arising out of the relationship between employer and employee. Instances of such disputes might include employee allegations that the employer did not pay wages due, or that an employment contract was not terminated by the correct amount of notice, or that the employer required the worker to perform work outside the job description in the worker's employment contract; or, conversely, an employer's claims for damages against employees on the grounds of willful or negligent damage. There are sixty such courts distributed throughout Austria.

The bench of a labor court is composed of one professional judge, who chairs the court, and two lay assessors; there is no jury. Austrian judges generally do not specialize in a particular branch of law; on the contrary, they compete for senior court positions, often moving from one branch of the law to another in the process. Professional judges are therefore generalists. The lay assessors, on the other hand, are nominated by the statutory organizations of employers and employees. For employee assessors, members of works councils often act in the position, but assessors in the superior courts are usually legally trained officials of the trade unions or of the chamber of labor. On the employers' side, individual employers occasionally act as assessors, but usually the senior staff of industrial or commercial establishments (frequently staff from personnel or legal departments) do so. Lay assessors are appointed for five years on a renewable appointment, and the office carries no remuneration.

Although the professional judge as chair of the bench is in charge of proceedings, judgment is given by all three members of the court by a majority decision. The lay assessors principally give the bench the benefit of their advice as specialists in the trade or industry concerned, leavening judgments with realism. The participation of lay assessors is also intended to ward off the impression that the courts might be prejudiced in favor of one or the other side of industry. The labor courts seek to influence litigant parties to come to terms, and most proceedings end in a compromise settlement rather than a formal judgment.

The procedure is simpler and faster than in ordinary civil proceedings. As in all civil litigation, there are no formal restrictions or rules of evidence. In addition, the litigants are not required to have legal representation, at least as far as proceedings of first and second instance are concerned. They may, however, choose to be represented by officials of the interest organizations, which provide free legal aid to their members. These officials, who are specialists in the field of labor law, thus appear in the labor courts in two different and seemingly incompatible functions: in some proceedings they act as lay assessors, in others they represent litigants. As a result of the free service that organizations provide their members with, the legal profession seldom concerns itself with labor law.

Judgments by a labor court may be contested by appeal, and appeal invalidates the finding of the original court. If the appellate court is required to hear a matter in labor law, it will sit as a special bench composed of three professional judges and two lay assessors. Fresh evidence may be submitted in appellate proceedings, although the courts at that level will, as a rule, concern themselves with points of law rather than with points of fact. Further appeals may be made to the Supreme Court of Judicature, if the value of the litigation exceeds a statutorily defined limit, or if the two lower courts have given divergent judgments. Before the Supreme Court the parties may neither plead their own cases nor be represented by anyone who is not a member of the Austrian bar. Appeals are heard again by a special bench of three judges and two lay assessors, and only points of law may be raised before the Supreme Court. Its findings are not subject to further appeal.

Judgments of the Supreme Court of Judicature are accorded a measure of importance that transcends their effect on the immediate issue. Austrian law recognizes no binding precedents, so each court is at liberty to depart from previous decisions in seemingly analogous cases. Nevertheless, the Supreme Court is extremely reluctant to deviate from its previous decisions. The reason for this attitude lies in the fact that both lawyers and laymen take their cues from the Supreme Court's judgments and transact their legal business in accordance with the principles underlying these judgments. The Supreme Court therefore refers to its own findings as authoritative and will cite them in support of a subsequent judgment. Although a complete reversal of legal view occurs very seldom, the court does occasionally deviate from previous judgments in points of detail or in its reasoning, and such deviations sometimes amount to a change in interpretation. Austrian courts usually will not admit that they have changed their interpretation of law. They usually contend that they are moving within the limits set by the framework of legislation and that they are now merely applying, in slightly modified form, legal views they have previously expressed.

It is worth noting, incidentally, that the courts have solved many problems to which legislation has failed to pay adequate attention. Examples serve to illustrate the point. It was the courts that developed the "no discrimination doctrine," which lays down that discrimination between single workers and their fellows gives rise to a claim for equality of treatment against the employer. Employers who give their staff benefits they are neither legally nor contractually bound to provide thereby assume the obligation to provide these benefits in the future; to avoid such a legal obligation, employers must make an explicit statement that no legal obligation can be inferred from their conduct each time they make the benefits in question available to their staff. Several employment contracts of limited duration between the same parties, in succession and without a considerable break between them, are in principle inadmissible, because such a practice may be intended merely to deny to employees certain rights based on long service. An employee who waives a claim to which he or she is entitled is regarded as acting under duress, and the waiver is viewed as meaningless. An employee who receives too much pay by mistake and spends it in good faith is not required to refund the excess to the employer. These and other rules are now firmly established, though they have no adequate basis in legislation. All stem from consistently applied court decisions.

There is no uniformity of procedure in the administration of labor law. Side by side with the labor courts are special administrative authorities, the previously mentioned conciliation departments, which adjudicate disputes arising where works councils are entitled to co-determination—for example, in matters of dismissals. Conciliation departments have been set up in each of the nine provinces; they discharge their quasi-judicial functions in committees, which include lay assessors nominated by the interest organizations. To all outward appearances, there is little difference between court and department. The latter's members are, however, denied the explicit privileges of the judiciary; they are not independent of the executive in the way that judges are, and they can be removed from office. Indeed, they are subject to the direction of the minister of social affairs, although no directives have been issued in recent years.

The procedure for deciding a case before an administrative authority such as a conciliation department is more elastic than the procedure in court. The most important point of difference is that a decision by a conciliation department comes into full effect at the time it is made. If it upholds a challenge to the validity of a dismissal notice, for example, the latter is null and void, and the employment contract continues in effect. If a conciliation department, on the motion of a party, rules that a works council election is invalid, a fresh election must be arranged immediately. The decision of a conciliation department may be appealed to the Administrative High Court, but appeal does not suspend the department's finding. Appeals to the Administrative High Court are none too frequent; the court is burdened with many cases and takes one to two years before it can issue a finding, while the problems involved in a particular case are usually of a pressing nature. Moreover, the Administrative High Court and the Supreme Court of Judicature will occasionally differ on their interpretation of identical facts.

For these and other reasons, the idea has been gaining popularity that this dual system should be reformed. Suggested alternatives include a single system for the jurisdiction of the labor courts and the adjudication of claims under social insurance law.

4

◊

SOCIAL PROGRAMS

A UNIVERSAL DEMAND AMONG WORKERS for increased security has grown steadily since 1945, and the boom conditions of the 1960s and 1970s favored those demands. The Socialist party took the lead in the field of social security immediately after the war. Referring to an impressive record in social policy in the 1920s—progress achieved in housing, education, and the provision of social services (particularly in care for mothers and children)—the Socialists resumed what the authoritarian Dollfuss government had forced the earlier Social Democratic party to abandon in 1933–34. So strong was public demand that the strongest political force in 1945, the Austrian People's party, also accepted the need for agressive social policy. Even today the two parties frequently argue over which deserves credit for having conceived specific social schemes.

During the Great Coalition of the two major political parties, which lasted from 1945 to 1966, disputes relating to social policy were occasionally responsible for dissolving Parliament and holding general elections. Social security and similar issues more often than not figured as central issues in election campaigns. Toward the end of 1952, for example, with economic growth clearly declining, Reinhard Kamitz, a nominee of the Austrian People's party who was then federal minister of finance, anticipated a drastic reduction in state revenue for the year 1953. To balance the budget for that year, he proposed cuts in two Socialist-controlled departments, the Federal Ministry of Social Affairs and the Ministry of Transport (which was also responsible for the administration of nationalized industries). Housing construction funds were to be reduced, and similar economies were to curtail the investment program of the Ministry of Transport, particularly in the nationalized sector. Kamitz also proposed that the state's contributions to the costs of pension insurance be reduced from 30 percent to 25 percent. Acrimonious discussions between the coalition parties led to the resignation of the government and to general elections in February 1953 in which the People's party lost three seats in Parliament and the Socialists gained six. Given the stability of Austrian politics at the time, this change in the composition of Parliament (then composed of 165 deputies) amounted to a veritable political landslide, and it signaled the sensitivity of the electorate to matters of social policy.

Social security systems had been operating in Western and Central Europe long before World War II. Benefits in the 1930s were relatively high, although, if only on account of the Great Depression, they bear no comparison with present-day standards. The roots of social security go back to the time of the industrial revolution. The first important step was taken in 1881 by the Bismarck government in Germany. There, for the first time, a comprehensive social insurance scheme was gradually developed. In 1883 the Austrian government, supported by Catholic and conservative forces, resolved to emulate the German example. Parliament passed legislation in 1887 that introduced an occupational injuries insurance scheme, and one year later enacted a program of sickness insurance. Both enactments were limited to manual laborers, and both leaned heavily on the German example. A pension scheme covering white-collar workers came into being in 1906, but the outbreak of World War I put an end to further attempts at reform.

The difficult years following 1918 could only favor the rapid development of social legislation. The state assumed responsibility for the livelihood of demobilized soldiers and for war veterans, as well as for widows and orphans whose breadwinners had died in active service. Lack of adequate nourishment, clothing, and heating in the last years of the war had played havoc with the health of the population, and tuberculosis and related diseases had become widespread. But acute shortages of funds permitted the adoption of only isolated assistance measures within the existing welfare and social services system. Moreover, widespread unemployment necessitated the introduction of an unemployment insurance scheme (1920).

In regard to old age pensions, the year 1935 saw the enactment of legislation providing for a uniform system of social security covering both white- and blue-collar workers. But the act was subject to the proviso that, for blue-collar workers, the system should only come into operation when the Austrian economy recovered from the depression. Such a recovery did not materialize during the First Republic. The incorporation of Austria into the German Reich in 1938 brought the introduction of German law concerning social insurance, which included old age pensions for manual laborers. Occupational injuries insurance was extended to cover the self-employed. In order to deprive the Ostmark, as the Austrian territory came to be called, of every vestige of a separate identity, Austrian law in the areas of poor relief and noncontributory benefits was gradually brought into line with or replaced by corresponding legal provisions of the German Reich.

After the war, Austria had no choice but to accept the continued validity of German law within its territory. However, as early as the autumn of 1945, a new government, ignoring the division of the country into four separate zones of occupation and claiming authority to represent the entire nation, came into being and began the work of reconstruction. This national government hastened to replace the alien law that the Nazis had imposed on the Austrian people with indigenous legislation.

The process of substituting Austrian for German social insurance law culminated in 1955 with the enactment of the General Social Insurance Act (*Allgemeines Sozialversicherungsgesetz*, or ASVG). The way had been prepared with legislation providing noncontributory benefits for the victims of the war and their survivors, and also those who had suffered persecution under fascist regimes, passed almost as soon as the Austrian state was resurrected in 1945. In response to conditions of the immediate post-war period, parliament passed a number of special public welfare enactments, particularly in the area of family welfare.

Austrian political and legal draftsmen could not ignore the comprehensive concept of social security that had evolved in Britain and the

United States during World War II. Austrians interpreted the principles enshrined in Article 22 of the United Nations Declaration of Human Rights as explicitly and implicitly advocating a drastic departure from the concept of selective care for specific groups in favor of measures beneficial to society as a whole. Accordingly, all persons, regardless of the nature of their pursuits, who are gainfully employed—not just selected groups such as civil servants—should be protected by social security and allied legislation. The state should work toward full employment, protecting jobs while protecting the social rights and interests of the working population. Ideas of this kind—they were worked out in detail in the Beveridge Report to the British government of 1942—have since exercised a decisive influence on Austrian social policy. Each successive government has given and still gives absolute priority to maintaining a system of full employment.

The departure from selective and group-specific measures won support from the overwhelming majority of Austrians. The self-employed have flocked to the idea of social security, wanting to be protected in the same manner and to the same extent as wage earners. As a result, about 97 percent of the population participates in the branch of social insurance that deals with sickness benefits, even though it by no means amounts to a national health service as understood by the British social welfare system. There is statutory protection against occupational injuries and diseases for virtually anyone who is gainfully employed or self-employed (with the exception of a few small groups such as lawyers and architects). The number of persons covered by pension insurance is also disproportionately high.

Why do Austrians stress the need for protection? The question is all the more interesting as Austria, despite its size, has for some time set the pace in introducing new employment models and fresh ideas about social security. Moreover, Austria plays an extremely important role in the work of international organizations whenever a question touching upon social security appears on their agendas.

As a result of two world wars, a worldwide depression, and occupation by different alien powers, two generations of Austrians forfeited virtually everything in the way of wealth that they and their forefathers had been able to accumulate. Feelings of utter helplessness stimulated them to join with others exposed to similar perils and hazards. Pooling their efforts, they spread the risks involved evenly among them and, accordingly, diminished the losses an individual would bear. Not long after the General Social Insurance Act introduced a distinct, comprehensive system of social security for wage earners, farmers and self-employed persons in commerce and industry began to clamor for similar protection. To satisfy the needs of these groups, legislation was enacted two years later. As with pension schemes for wage earners, pension systems for the self-employed require subsidy from the public purse.

Principles of Social Welfare Legislation

Social welfare, in its widest sense, includes not only social security, health services, and the care of the elderly and the disabled, but also facilities designed to promote education and housing. The system can be split into three classes of legislation. The first, social insurance law, is designed to provide payments from a pool of prior contributions. The second involves noncontributory benefits, available to individuals without contribution conditions. (For example, the state accepts a duty to provide for disabled war veterans.) The third covers the field of public assistance. The authorities grant to persons whose resources are insufficient to meet their basic needs a measure of relief on an ex gratia basis, but the beneficiary has no legal entitlement to the relief concerned.

These three classes of legislation may, for want of better terms in English, be called, respectively, the insurance principle, the subsistence principle, and the relief principle. The reader should understand that in practice no area of social legislation involves the exclusive application of any one of these principles. Nevertheless, each principle puts a distinctive stamp on measures in a particular area.

When Austrians refer to social insurance, they usually mean insurance against sickness and occupational injuries and pensions (the last also includes provisions for invalidism and death). The insurance principle, according to which resources are pooled to address common risk in the presence of certain statutorily defined circumstances, insures people automatically and by operation of law, whether they want it or not. Such insurance obligates the payment of contributions. In addition to the employed person's contributions, employers are also required to contribute, usually in an equal measure. In the case of self-employed persons in commerce and industry and farmers, the state acts the part of the employer and matches the individual's contribution. If—as is the case with all pension insurance schemes—receipts from contributions fall short of the amount needed for the payment of benefits, the state guarantees the difference. If there is a deficit in sickness or occupational injuries insurance, on the other hand, contributions must be raised or benefits must be reduced to wipe out the deficit. (In the case of farmers, the state accepts a measure of responsibility for costs.) Employers' contributions alone finance occupational injuries insurance.

As a corollary to the insured person's duty to pay contributions, he or she is entitled to claim benefit from the "social insurance carriers," as the administering organizations are called. Conversely, these carriers are obliged to make available such benefit as may be appropriate in the circumstances. The claim to benefit is a legal entitlement, which may be enforced by court action.

The carriers for sickness, occupational injuries, and pension insurance are autonomous bodies; that is, subject to a certain amount of statutory control, they are self-governing. Thus social insurance is administered by representatives of the insured and, in those schemes that cater to wage earners, representatives of the employers. The state confines itself to overseeing the legality of the carriers' acts and decisions. Unemployment insurance, on the other hand, is directly administered by the public authorities.

All Austrian insurance schemes are dynamic in the sense that both contributions and benefits are regularly revalued to bring them into line with current wage trends.

Law based on the subsistence principle, unlike social insurance law, is administered by the public authorities. The persons affected have no, or at most very little, say. In terms of financial impact the most important piece of subsistence legislation relates to the civil service. All public servants are outside the scope of statutory social pension insurance. The state or whatever public authority employs them makes provision to meet those contingencies covered by statutory pension insurance in the private sector.

Subsistence legislation also provides financial assistance to victims of special circumstances, such as war invalids and their survivors, persons who sustain injuries while serving with the Austrian armed forces, and victims of political persecution between 1934 and 1945. Legislation also helps victims of crime and persons who suffer aftereffects from certain kinds of vaccination. (Through the Vaccination Injuries Act of 1973 the state compensates those who suffer bodily injury from vaccinations. The injured person and, where applicable, his or her survivors are entitled to benefits in kind and in cash.) Moreover, the state pays provisional alimony when the person obliged to make such payments fails to do so. Thus the Advance of Maintenance Payments Act of 1976 provides for payment, by and on the authority of the courts, of maintenance due to a minor, up to a specified limit. The local youth office then attempts to recover payment from the liable person.

The relief principle in the area of public assistance is subsidiary to all other forms of social welfare. It applies only if no other means of aid, under either the insurance or under the subsistence principles, is available and if self-help is not practicable. Both social insurance and schemes involving the application of the subsistence principle are regulated by central (federal) legislation, which applies uniformly throughout Austria. Public assistance, on the other hand, is a matter for the several provinces.

One further Austrian peculiarity deserves mention. Employers usually pay all employees two extra bonuses per year, each being equal to one month's wages. All cash benefits provided under the social security system, insofar as they are intended to compensate for loss of earnings, are also paid fourteen times a year.

In addition to social programs, legislation also deals with grants. Virtually every citizen benefits, at one time or another, from one of the many grants available. Usually in cash, grants fall into three broad classes: grants intended to ease the financial strain arising from family commitments; grants calculated to facilitate education and occupational training; and grants given with a view to securing and maintaining a high level of employment. Most grants do not depend upon prior contributions, and even where they do, the size of previous contributions bears little relation to the value of the benefits. For the Austrian population as a whole, these grants, because of their impact on the standard of living, have assumed an importance almost equal to that of social insurance.

A certain amount of overlap in the structure of social services is inevitable, and by no means rare. Moreover, benefits that provide special aid in special circumstances may have inadvertent effects. For example, the maternity benefit payable to unmarried mothers and the period for which it may be claimed (e.g., the amount of maternity leave) are often greater than the same benefits for married mothers. Parents may thus delay their intended marriage until they have obtained the special benefits associated with unmarried motherhood. Such unanticipated results of welfare facilities are the consequence of the rapid expansion of the social welfare system during the economic prosperity of the 1960s and 1970s—an expansion so rapid it lacked coordination. The rapid increase in social welfare legislation also rendered it virtually impossible to subject the whole complex of social policy to systematic scientific research.

The Austrian welfare state, constructed under conditions of prosperity, aims to provide the widest possible range of social services to promote the health and well-being of its citizens. But the huge mass of legal enactments regarding social welfare is so confusing that determining their impact on the redistribution of wealth and income is impossible. After twenty-five years of placid acquiescence, financial bottlenecks in the system—above all, in the field of social insurance—coupled with a growing weakness of the economy, have begun to revive discussion about where the boundaries of the welfare state ought to be drawn.

As mentioned earlier, social insurance as generally understood involves pensions and insurance against sickness and occupational injuries. The core of the Austrian system of social security, these programs merit a chapter of their own.

UNEMPLOYMENT INSURANCE AND RELATED SCHEMES

A system of unemployment insurance has been in operation in Austria since 1920. The law that regulates the system is contained in the Unemployment Insurance Act of 1949 (as amended and consolidated, it was last repromulgated as the "Unemployment Insurance Act of 1977").

When Austrians speak of social insurance, they usually omit unemployment insurance, even though unemployment insurance resembles social insurance schemes in that it is compulsory and participation in it is automatic. The reason Austrians make the distinction is that unemployment insurance is administered by the state, whereas social insurance proper is administered by autonomous bodies—that is, by those insured together, where appropriate, with their employers. The state authorities that administer unemployment insurance are the local employment exchanges, the regional employment exchanges, and, at the top level, the Federal Ministry of Social Affairs.

Unemployment benefits are intended to compensate insured persons against loss of earnings caused by unemployment. Unemployment pay and subsistence allowances were originally the only benefits available under the scheme. Other benefits have since come to be included in the system: advance payments for pensions, maternity leave allowance, and a special subsistence allowance for unmarried mothers. The receipt of unemployment benefits automatically enrolls the recipient in Austria's statutory health insurance scheme, the recipient's contributions being paid out of unemployment insurance.

Scope of Unemployment Insurance

Persons subject to compulsory health insurance are also automatically enrolled in the unemployment insurance scheme, unless they are specifically exempted (e.g., established civil servants and pensioners). To register a person for health insurance is to register him or her for unemployment insurance. The Regional Sickness Fund (*Gebietskrankenkasse*), responsible for administering health insurance in the area in which the insured person's place of work is located, is charged with collecting the contributions payable under the health insurance scheme, on the one hand, and under the unemployment insurance scheme, on the other.

Registration and Withdrawal

The responsibility for registering an employee for unemployment insurance with the Regional Sickness Fund, or for notifying the fund of an employee's withdrawal from the scheme, rests with the employer. Employers are obliged to give the fund all the information the fund requires, and violators are subject to penalty.

The state advances the funds required for the payment of benefits under unemployment insurance, but ultimately these benefits are paid for by insured persons' contributions, by the contributions of employers, and by the state out of general taxation. (Maternity leave allowance is a special case, partly paid for by the Family Burden Equalization Scheme, described later in this chapter). Employer and employee contributions are graduated and related to the employed person's earnings. Contributions are levied at 4.4 percent of the employed person's earnings, up to a maximum contribution ceiling, and are payable in equal shares by the employer and the employee.

Benefits

To be entitled to unemployment benefits, an insured person must be unemployed, capable of work, and available for employment. The insured person must also satisfy the prescribed contribution conditions. Unemployment benefits may be claimed only for a limited period (twelve or thirty weeks).

There are two main contribution conditions for unemployment benefit eligibility. Before the first spell of unemployment, the person concerned must have been insured for a minimum of fifty-two weeks within the two years immediately preceding the claim. For each subsequent claim, it is sufficient for the insured person to show an insurance record of twenty weeks of work within the twelve months before the new claim. Periods of insurable employment that were completed outside Austria but in a country with which Austria has a reciprocal agreement on social security covering unemployment insurance (e.g., the Federal Republic of Germany, Switzerland, Italy, and Great Britain) are treated as if they had been completed within Austria.

Unemployment pay is due from the first day of joblessness, provided that it is applied for on that day; otherwise, it is due from the day on which the claim is made. An insured person whose employment is terminated for cause is disqualified from receiving benefits for the first four weeks after termination.

Unemployment pay consists of a basic benefit plus supplements for the insured person's dependents. The basic amount is related to wage levels and is calculated with reference to the insured person's gross earnings during the last four weeks of work. The gap between the insured person's gross earnings and the basic benefit is less in the case of low-paid workers (for whom the basic benefit may be as high as 58 percent of gross earnings) than in the case of workers in higher income brackets (for whom the basic benefit may be as low as 40 percent of gross earnings). Supplements are paid for the unemployed person's dependents if he or she provides them with maintenance and they have no income of their own.

In 1983 the average monthly income was about S10,600 (10,600 schillings), and the maximum rate for basic unemployment benefits was S7,544 per month. Supplements of S480 were paid for each dependent. Basic benefits and supplements may not, in the aggregate, exceed 80 percent of the insured person's most recent gross earnings. A married man with one child therefore received in 1983 a maximum basic benefit of S7,544 a month plus supplements of S960. If his spouse had income of her own, he would receive a supplement of only S480. Unemployment benefits are payable for twelve weeks, or up to thirty weeks where the claimant has an insurance record of suitable length.

Unemployment benefits must be claimed in person from the local employment exchange. Employment exchange decisions about claims can be appealed to the regional employment exchange, whose decision is final. No further administrative appeal is possible.

There are certain limitations on the eligibility for unemployment benefits; the most important affect pensioners. An unemployed person who has applied for a pension under the pensions insurance scheme is automatically disqualified from receiving unemployment benefits, as are persons who already receive a pension (or any of several other social benefits). But the procedure for determining pension rights usually takes some time. As a result, the local employment exchange may, if a pension is likely to be awarded, pay an advance out of the funds of the unemployment insurance scheme against later repayment from a backdated pension.

After the twelve or thirty weeks of unemployment benefits expire, an insured person who is still out of work is entitled to claim subsistence allowance if he or she is living "in distressed circumstances." Subsistence allowance is restricted to Austrian citizens who are unemployed, capable of work, and available for work. A person is deemed to be living in distressed circumstances if his or her income, together with the income of those relatives who are legally obliged to maintain him or her, is insufficient to provide the necessities of life. Subsistence allowance is paid at the rate of 92 percent of the appropriate unemployment pay, or at 100 percent of unemployment pay if the claimant is the sole breadwinner of a family. There is no time limit on the payment of subsistence allowance.

Maternity leave allowance is subject to several special conditions, codified in the Mothers' Protection Act of 1979. The act requires a pregnant woman to abstain from paid work from eight weeks before the expected date of confinement until the end of the eighth week following delivery. (The period after confinement is twelve weeks for multiple births, premature delivery, and delivery by cesarean section.) To receive compensation for lost earnings, women workers may claim a maternity allowance from their health insurance carrier. Employers, furthermore, are obliged upon request to grant unpaid leave of absence for a maximum of one year starting with the confinement. After maternity allowance has run out, a new mother can claim maternity leave allowance, which is payable from unemployment insurance. Without this maternity leave allowance, many mothers would be unable to take advantage of their right to an unpaid leave of absence from work.

Maternity leave allowance is paid only if the claimant is able to satisfy the contribution conditions that apply for the receipt of unemployment pay. Furthermore, the woman concerned must be on unpaid maternity leave from her place of work, and she must personally look after her newborn child. The allowance is intended to enable mothers to take care of their children for at least the first year of life. Maternity leave allowance is not related to level of earnings; it is paid at a flat rate. The size of the allowance is fixed year by year to conform with the current economic situation. In 1983 the allowance amounted to S5,560 per month for unmarried mothers and S3,717 for married mothers. The allowance is payable from the day on which maternity allowance expires until the child's first birthday.

Unmarried mothers receive greater benefits than do married mothers. Single mothers who cannot go out of the home to work because they need to look after their children are entitled to a special subsistence allowance after their maternity leave allowance has run out. To qualify, an unmarried mother must be an Austrian citizen, living in distressed circumstances, and unable to provide alternative nursing facilities for her child. This special allowance is payable at the same rate as ordinary subsistence allowance. This special subsistence allowance is payable from the child's first birthday (when regular maternity leave allowance expires) until the child's fourth birthday.

Unemployment insurance is supplemented by the provisions of various other legal enactments. If unemployment insurance makes provision to meet the contingencies of joblessness, three acts look to combat the phenomenon of unemployment, to assist the unemployed, and to protect wage earners against losses arising from their employers' insolvency.

Employment Promotion Act

The Employment Promotion Act (*Arbeitsmarktfoerderunggesetz*) is intended both to maintain high levels of employment and to forestall the dangers of widespread unemployment. The act entered into operation on January 1, 1969, and it provides a wide range of services: occupational guidance for the choice of a career or a career change, assistance to people looking for jobs and apprenticeships, information about suitable workers for employers, and help to people in adapting to specific jobs or apprenticeships. Citizens who use these various services do so of their own volition—none is compulsory. Moreover, the authorities are required by law to treat in the strictest confidence any personal data they may gather in helping individuals.

Authorities that provide employment services are under a duty to ascertain, one year in advance, the likely supply of and demand for labor in the areas they serve. Using these projections, the Federal Ministry of Social Affairs then plans for aggregate and long-run changes in the national labor market.

A wide range of financial grants designed to assist employment schemes has been introduced over the years. These grants are intended, above all, to provide workers with better qualifications and new skills, as well as to pave the way for a change of career when such a change is necessary. Grants also serve to alleviate hardships arising from increased living costs, job-related commuting expenses, moving costs associated with a career change, special work clothes and equipment, and similar items. Loans and subsidies also ease the financial strains involved. Moreover, to offset short-term fluctuations in employment, grants can be made to employers to avoid reductions in their work force. Even the mere threat of unemployment in the foreseeable future can trigger grants to employers. Through the medium of a special advisory council at the Federal Ministry of Social Affairs, on which both sides of industry are equally represented, employers and employees alike have a say in the various schemes that promote employment.

Austrian employment promotion policies makes use of an interesting "early warning system." An amendment to the Employment Promotion Act in 1979 empowers the federal minister for social affairs to require all employers in specific sectors of the economy to notify local employment exchanges of their intention to lay off a substantial proportion of their work force no later than four weeks before the first worker is given notice. Employers must give the employment exchange the names of employees who are to be dismissed, their ages, and sexes, as well as the kinds of work in which they are employed. Individual employees cannot legally be terminated without such prior notification.

This early warning system gives the authorities time to make arrangements to prevent large-scale unemployment, either by making grants available to the employer or by finding alternative employment for the workers. Employment exchanges are now equipped with automatic data-processing machines that enable them to call up job opportunities nationwide. The costs of employment promotion measures, including the administrative expenses involved, are covered by general taxation and by the funds available from the unemployment insurance scheme.

Special Benefit Act

The Special Benefit Act (*Sonderunterstuetzungsgesetz*), introduced in 1967, was originally intended to deal only with the social problems faced by elderly workers when collieries closed. Now considerably broader in scope, the Special Benefit Act is intended to bridge the interval between work and early retirement for elderly workers who are laid off and cannot find alternative employment. Today two classes of employees benefit from the measures provided in the act: first, employees who lose their jobs because their employers' businesses close down or shrink in size "in connection with economic difficulties occasioned by Austria's association with the EEC or by major changes in the pattern of international competition, or by a process of reorganization or restructuring." Such workers are eligible for special benefits if they are out of work and cannot be found suitable employment, provided that male workers are when their employment ends at least fifty-five, and female workers are at least fifty years of age. The second class of beneficiaries includes persons who are unemployed for any reason and who are, when their employment ends or upon receipt of unemployment benefits or subsistence allowance, fifty-nine years of age (for women, fifty-four). To be eligible, a person must in the previous twenty-five years have been in insurable employment for at least 180 months and have an insurance record showing no fewer than 180 months in pensions insurance. Moreover, to be eligible for special benefits such persons must be both capable of work and available for further employment.

The size of the special benefit in the first class of employees is equal to the invalid's pension that would have been received if invalidism had terminated their employment. Persons in the second class are entitled to a 25 percent increment to the basic unemployment benefit, though the basic benefit plus the increment may in the aggregate not exceed the beneficiary's notional pension or 80 percent of most recent gross earnings, whichever is less.

The recipients of special benefits are covered by health insurance. The award of special benefits is in the hands of the local employment exchange. Special benefits cease on the day on which the beneficiary becomes entitled to an old age pension. Disputes between claimants and authorities are resolved through the procedural provisions contained in social insurance legislation.

The costs arising from the payment of special benefits are covered partly by the funds allocated to the unemployment insurance scheme and partly by general taxation.

Protection of Wages in Bankruptcy Act

The Protection of Wages in Bankruptcy Act (*Insolvenz-Engeltsicherungsgesetz*), one of the more recent pieces of Austrian legislation, went into effect on January 1, 1978. It was prompted by awareness of the risks suffered by workers whose employer becomes insolvent. An employer's lack of funds, or indebtedness may jeopardize workers' legitimate claims to arrears of wages or to severance pay. The act ensures that workers' financial claims against their employers will be satisfied.

In order to obtain the benefits provided by the act, employees are required to notify the local employment exchange of their claims and to submit evidence corroborating their claims. If the employment exchange finds the claim or claims to be justified, it will proceed to award what is known under the act as "insolvency deficiency money" to the claimants. Needy claimants who submit prima facie evidence in support of their claims may obtain an advance on such payments. The amounts involved are paid out of a special fund set up for the purpose. Insolvency deficiency payments transfer workers' claims against their employer to the fund. The fund then tries in its own name to recover the amount it has disbursed from the employer. The risk that claims may not be enforceable is borne by the fund, not the workers.

The costs of the scheme are defrayed partly by a special increment of 0.5 percent to employers' contributions under unemployment insurance and partly by what the fund succeeds in recovering from defaulting employers. (It should be noted that under Austrian law formal bankruptcy does not relieve the bankrupt of obligations toward creditors.)

THE SUBSISTENCE PRINCIPLE IN WELFARE LAW

The characteristic features of legislation inspired by the subsistence principle have been described earlier, when we noted that subsistence law is split into numerous separate fields. The following schemes seek to implement the subsistence principle in the realm of social welfare. The reader will understand, of course, that the term "welfare" is construed here very widely and includes the provision of benefits not normally understood as falling under that heading.

War Invalids

Pensions and allowances for Austrian citizens disabled or bereaved through war or service in the armed forces of the Dual Monarchy, the First Republic, and the German Reich (between March 13, 1938 and May 8, 1945) are payable under the provisions of the War Invalids' Benefits Act of 1949. In addition, the act provides such benefits in kind as medical care, rehabilitation facilities, and the supply of prosthetics and orthopedic appliances.

The size of pension is determined by the war invalid's disablement—the extent to which earning capacity is diminished as the result of a war or a service injury. To be eligible for a pension an invalid must have had his or her earning capacity diminished by at least 25 percent. Ninety percent disablement is regarded as rendering an individual totally unfit for work. The basic pension for total disablement was S3,550 per month in 1983, and the size of the pension for partial disablement varies according to the degree of disablement. Degree is assessed by comparing the war invalid's condition with that of a healthy person of the same age and sex. The amount of basic pension is low, but a wide range of supplementary allowances is available. The main allowances are for constant nursing attendance and for medical care.

Pensions are also payable to war widows, war orphans, and the parents of war invalids. The survivors of a war invalid are also entitled to receive the constant attendance allowance if they are helpless, or a dietary allowance if they have to keep to a diet. Widows, orphans, and parents who are entitled to benefits automatically become insured against sickness. Their contributions to the health insurance scheme amount to 3 percent of their pensions. In 1983 nearly 165,000 war invalids were still receiving these benefits, at a cost of approximately S6 billion. According to Austrian practice, all pensions and allowances are paid fourteen times a year and are annually increased to stay roughly in line with percentage movements in average earnings.

Persons Disabled While Serving with the Armed Forces

Austrian citizens who suffer injuries while in active service with the armed forces of the Second Republic ("service injuries") are eligible for benefits provided in the Federal Forces Benefits Act. Introduced in 1964, the act has since been frequently amended, mainly to expand and improve the range of benefits available. The act now covers injuries suffered while reporting for duty or during deployment, as well as injuries sustained by civilians and caused by military activities. The last category, known as "equivalent service injuries," is treated in the same way as service injuries proper, provided that the injured person was not at fault in the incident.

Conditions for the award of benefits, and the types of benefits covered, under the act are the same as those under the War Invalids' Benefits Act. In 1983 nearly 1,000 persons were entitled to claim benefits under the scheme, at a cost of approximately S40 million.

Victims of Political Persecution

As early as 1946 a Political Victims' Welfare Act was passed by Parliament to provide some measure of compensation and assistance to individuals who had been victimized by the Austrian authorities or the National Socialist party between March 4, 1933 and May 9, 1945, for political reasons or reasons related to their racial descent, their religious persuasion, or their nationality.

Both the value and extent of the benefits in question are manifold; they range from the right to privileged treatment in matters of taxation and trade licensing to the right to claim special "political victims' pensions," and the provision of medical facilities and child care. Some benefits are related to income; on the whole, benefits relate to the extent of the victim's suffering (and, of course, its effects on health and earning power), on the one hand, and to the victim's needs, on the other.

Surviving dependents of victims (usually widows and orphans, more rarely parents) are also entitled to benefit from the act. The definition of survivors who are entitled to claim is broad and includes women who cohabited with male victims as their wives and men who cohabited with female victims as their husbands. A death grant is due to the next of kin of deceased victims. Victims who are not enrolled in any of the statutory health insurance schemes can demand that the authorities concerned with their welfare provide them with all health care facilities that health insurance schemes provide to enrolled persons.

Political victims receive benefits that, under certain statutorily defined circumstances, may be claimed as a right. Benefits are of course noncontributory and are covered by general taxation. The pensions and allowance system is dynamic. It is reviewed every year, and benefits are brought into line with current economic conditions automatically, without special legislation. In conformity with Austrian practice, pensions and allowances are paid fourteen times a year.

Special mention should be made of the rights of victims of political persecution to pensions. The effect of these rights is an almost gratuitous pension award. In 1983 the number of beneficiaries was about forty-six hundred; the costs involved in the provision of benefits under the act amounted to approximately S240 million.

Victims of Crime

Before 1972 the only remedy available to victims of violent crimes was to institute civil proceedings against the culprit. But awards of damages were seldom paid because of defendant's lack of funds to satisfy the judgment. Victims could claim some measure of compensation from benefits and services under the social insurance scheme—if they were enrolled. Those victims who were not insured had to prove they were destitute before they could receive public assistance.

A criminal injuries compensation scheme has been in effect in Austria since 1972. Cash benefits are assessed according to the amount of earnings lost as a result of the crime. Benefits in kind are similar to those provided under the War Invalids' Benefits Act.

Only Austrian citizens are eligible to claim benefit; they must have sustained bodily injuries or the loss of physical or mental faculties as the result of an offense punishable by more than six months in prison. Compensation may be claimed for medical costs and for lost earnings. Benefit, incidentally, depends not on the conviction of the person or persons who caused the injury but on the fact of the injury itself. A victim's survivors are entitled to dependents' benefits if his or her death was demonstrably due to crime.

Compensation is payable for lost earnings, but caps are set on the maximum amounts payable under the act. Allowances for constant attendance and blindness may be awarded, and a wide range of benefits includes the provision of medical, dental, and hospital treatment as well as the supply of drugs and orthopedic and prosthetic appliances. These benefits are supplied within the framework of health insurance, and the state covers costs.

Benefits are due from the date of injury, provided that a claim is submitted within six months, and the benefit in question ceases when the conditions prescribed for its award cease to apply. The state stands subrogated to the victim's claim for damages, and it may attempt to recoup its payments to the victim from the offender. Through 1983 benefits had been provided to approximately one hundred people at a cost to the state of about S5 million a year.

GRANTS

The variety of grants available makes their classification difficult. Some grants aim to promote family welfare, such as the several benefits provided under the Family Burden Equalization Scheme, the Housing Allowances Act of 1961, the Dwelling Construction Promotion Act of 1968, and the Dwellings Improvement Act of 1969. Clearly intended to stimulate education are the Studies Promotion Act of 1969 and the Pupils' Allowances Act of 1979. Grants introduced to maintain high levels of employment have already been mentioned in connection with the unemployment insurance system of which grants form an integral part. Such is the diversity of grants that it is no exaggeration to say that virtually every citizen is entitled to claim a grant of some sort.

The Family Burden Equalization Scheme, as its name implies, aims to equalize the financial burdens that fall upon persons with large family commitments, on the one hand, and those without such commitments or with lesser commitments, on the other. The scheme started in the immediate postwar period. In 1950 wage earners became entitled to child allowances, financed from contributions paid by their employers. Four years later, self-employed persons were also included in the allowances system. As a result of changes in taxation, the Equalization Fund for Family Allowances (which had meanwhile been established by statute) became financially so strong that it became possible not only to increase the size of the allowances but also to introduce new benefits, such as free school books and travel subsidies for students' journeys between home and their schools or colleges. The fund has repeatedly addressed tasks that by no stretch of the imagination could be said to bear upon the problem of "equalizing" burdens in the original sense; for example, the fund now covers part of the costs of providing accident insurance for students. The fund's growing responsibilities, financial and otherwise, in fields beyond its avowed purposes (that is, the extent to which funds that Parliament allocates to the furthering of family welfare may be applied to other ends) has provoked much controversy between government and opposition in recent years.

To be entitled to benefit the claimant must be either an Austrian citizen or have been employed for at least three months as a wage earner within Austria. Austrian family allowance is not payable to claimants who are entitled to a similar allowance from another country.

In general, family allowance may be claimed for children up to the age of twenty-seven; there is no such age limit in the case of disabled children who became disabled before reaching the age of twenty-seven. The right to claim allowance lies with the person to whose household the child belongs, but children over the age of sixteen may claim the allowance for themselves. The amount of the allowance depends on the number and age of children in the family concerned. In 1983 family allowance was paid at the rate of S1,000 a month for each child under ten and S1,200 a month for each child over ten. In the case of severely disabled children the rates were S2,200 or S2,400 a month, depending on age.

Wage earners receive a family allowance from their employers. Recipients of pensions and other social benefits receive such an allowance from the proper authority or insurance carrier. Self-employed persons are paid a family allowance by the fiscal authorities. The costs involved are ultimately met by the fund.

The fund, as noted, provides travel grants for students and free school books; it also provides confinement grants. On the delivery of a child, any woman who is an Austrian citizen or has been resident in the country for at least three years is entitled to a confinement grant. As of 1983 the grant is a nonrecurrent payment of S2,000. If the woman has submitted to certain medical examinations during her pregnancy, the amount is increased to S8,000 and is paid when the child is one week old. Confinement grants, in addition to their effects on family planning, are also intended to lower the rate of infant mortality. Thus a further S8,000 is awarded if the child undergoes specified medical examinations in the first twelve months of life, and a further S3,000 if the child is given further medical tests in the second year. Tests required to satisfy the criteria for the award of these various payments are specified by the health authorities.

The scheme is financed from various sources. Employers are required to contribute to the fund an amount equal to 4.5 percent of the wages and salaries they pay. That requirement provides about two-thirds of the funds's resources. These contributions are supplemented by grants out of general taxation, by subsidies paid by the provincial governments, by contributions paid under the unemployment insurance scheme, and by a statutorily defined proportion of the revenue derived from taxes on land and landed estates. Total expenditures of the Equalization Fund in 1983 were about S35 billion—8.8 percent of the total federal budget.

The Dwellings Construction Promotion Act and the Dwellings Improvement Act also aim to promote family welfare, inasmuch as the provision of residential accommodation, the improvement of housing conditions, and the lowering of housing costs (rentals) are intended to benefit the family as a unit rather than individual members of the community. The former act also makes provision for the payment of grants, though the grants are related to income. The act seeks to stimulate the modernization of existing housing stock that warrants preservation, as well as the improvement of small- and medium-size apartments. Grants provided under the act reduce the rate of interest on loans raised for the purpose of financing modernization and improvement.

The Studies Promotion Act makes provision for the award of grants to needy students who are able to show good progress in their studies. Special grants, which are intended to help parents pay private tuition fees, are available under the terms of the Pupils Allowances Act; these grants are related to income and depend upon the pupil's progress in his or her studies.

PUBLIC ASSISTANCE

Apart from cases where the provision of the bare necessities of life is at stake, the law on public assistance does not recognize a legal right to benefit. Benefits provided are of course not matched by any corresponding individual contributions. The law merely provides funds to individuals who need such assistance. The forms of assistance to the needy under various enactments are so numerous and so comprehensive that the specific requirements of each individual case can be met. Thus public assistance provides a safety net of support for all those who, for whatever reason, cannot claim benefits under other social programs and are incapable of providing for themselves.

Various enactments also make provision for the adoption of preventive and follow-up measures. The aim is eventually to place needy persons in a position in which they can support themselves. A person is deemed to stand in need of support if unable to provide self and family with the bare necessities of life and unable to qualify for social insurance and other mandatory social benefits to an extent that would provide these bare necessities. The person concerned is, however, expected to contribute to the best of his or her abilities. When determining the degree of need, account is taken of the value of any property assets as well as the person's legal obligation to provide maintenance of certain close relatives. Welfare authorities that render financial or other assistance to a needy person stand subrogated to his or her claim for maintenance against near relatives, though the authorities in recent years have only sparingly exercised the right to recover their outlays from close relatives.

The provision of cash benefits obviously represents the most conspicuous feature of the public assistance system. The size of these cash payments is subject to statutorily defined limits; however, these limits may be exceeded in individual cases that warrant special consideration. As pointed out earlier, benefits for the bare necessities of life are claimed as a right, and a decision by the authorities that is adverse to the claimant may be contested by appeal. The authorities, however, have virtually unfettered power to grant or refuse assistance in other circumstances; the authorities are also empowered to grant assistance when the bare necessities of life are not at stake. Assistance may be given in cash or in kind; the provision of personal services is also admissible and in practice quite common. The range of services and benefits in kind varies from province to province, and it may include the provision of medication, drugs, and orthopedic appliances, hospitalization, family grants, advice and guidance, vacation and convalescent grants, fuel, and many other items. The recipient of such benefits is not required to reimburse the authorities for the costs incurred.

As a result of the wide range of benefits provided under social insurance and the tight-knit net of social welfare measures that may be claimed as rights, public assistance has in recent years lost much of its former importance. In the whole of Austria, some forty thousand persons are permanently receiving public assistance. Nevertheless, in comparison with the former poor law system, the resources providing help in emergencies have conspicuously increased both in number and in scope. As a result, to implement their several public assistance systems, the nine provinces spend approximately S4 billion a year.

5

◇

SOCIAL INSURANCE

SOCIAL INSURANCE IS at the very core of the social security system. Austrians use the term "social insurance" to mean only health, occupational injury, and pension insurance. Health insurance is intended to meet the contingencies of illness as well as the special needs of pregnant women; occupational injury insurance assists those incapable of work because of occupational injuries and diseases; and pension insurance makes provision for the payment of benefits to those whose capacity for work is reduced as well as for pensions in the case of old age or death. These insurance schemes are known as separate insurance "branches."

Austrians thus construe the meaning of social insurance rather more restrictively than is usual in international parlance. The main reason is that unemployment insurance is organized differently from health, occupational injury, and pension insurance, which are administered by the persons insured and, where applicable, their employers. As a consequence, the administering organizations enjoy a large measure of autonomy and freedom from governmental interference. By contrast, unemployment insurance is in the hands of governmental authorities.

This arrangement reflects the fact that, to all intents and purposes, the state enjoys a monopoly in the area of job procurement. It is the government that directs job seekers to potential employers and supplies employers with suitable staff, and it does so within the framework of the unemployment insurance scheme. (Private employment agencies are strictly limited in Austria, and they are at most of minor importance.)

The basic principles of social insurance are codified in the General Social Insurance Act (*Allgemeines Sozialversicherungsgesetz*, the ASVG). It went into operation on January 1, 1956, the culmination of a decade in which Austrian legislation had gradually dismantled German law and adjusted benefits to the changing value of the schilling. The years since 1956 have seen the expansion, step by step, of social insurance to include the self-employed, including farmers. Benefits have been improved in various ways, and the magnitude of benefits has slowly been tied to current wage trends.

Like all countries in Western Europe, Austria made tremendous progress in social insurance during the 1960s and 1970s. The self-employed had previously regarded social insurance as a protective system appropriate only to wage earners. But the increase in benefits, as well as the replacement of the "flat rate" with earnings-related and inflation-protected benefits, made the system more attractive to them. In the course of the last twenty-five years free-lance journalists, some artists, medical practitioners, veterinary surgeons, pharmacists, and others have been included in the system, mostly at their own request and in special arrangements that recognize their special needs. Currently some 97 percent of the population enjoy the protection of the statutory health insurance scheme. Only those who are gainfully employed can enroll in the industrial injury and pension insurance schemes (provided that the employment concerned is not altogether outside the realm of social insurance, as, for example, the legal profession), but the number of persons so enrolled is not significantly lower than the numbers covered by health insurance. Given the wide scope of the Austrian social security system, it can be maintained with some justification that social insurance in Austria amounts to national insurance.

PRINCIPLES AND CONCEPTS OF AUSTRIAN SOCIAL INSURANCE

Before describing the several areas of Austrian social insurance, it is necessary to expound the principles underlying the country's system and to explain its fundamental concepts. The responsibility for social insurance, for both its legislation and execution, falls exclusively on the federal authorities; insofar as the provinces are concerned in social insurance law, they act on behalf of, and subject to direction by, the Federal Ministry of Social Affairs. The provinces are responsible to the federal minister for social affairs for any act or any omission on their part. The minister is in turn politically responsible in matters of social insurance to Parliament for both ministerial and provincial conduct.

The provincial authorities are nevertheless involved, in a somewhat roundabout way, in the development of social insurance legislation. Like numerous other institutions and organizations, they are entitled to present their views on any draft bill prepared by the federal minister for social affairs before the bill may come to Parliament for formal adoption. Provincial authorities, however, have no power of direct intervention. Similarly, where the implementation of law is entrusted to insurance carriers, the carriers, if they discharge quasi-governmental functions (e.g., if they make decisions as to a person's liability for insurance, or if they admit or disallow claims for benefits), also act as agents of the minister. The minister likewise bears political responsibility for the manner in which the carriers discharge their functions.

Political responsibility for social insurance thus lies at the federal level. But centralization of responsibility does not imply uniform organization; indeed, self-administration is the second pillar on which Austrian social insurance rests. There are a variety of social insurance carriers, totally independent of one another, that administer social insurance programs for different occupational groups. There are five major groups of insured persons: white-collar workers, blue-collar workers, established civil servants (*Beamte*), farmers, and other self-employed people. The principle of self-administration implies that social insurance is administered by representatives of the insured and their employers. These representatives must apply current law, but they are not subject to direction by state authorities, who merely supervise their conduct. The management of the affairs of the carrier, and thereby the execution of the law directly affecting claimants, is entrusted to a board of directors similar in structure and functions to boards that manage private companies. The majority of seats on the boards of carriers that cater to wage earners usually go to employees' representatives; employers' representatives, on the other hand, hold the majority of seats on the carriers' supervisory boards. (Voting on these various boards, and in particular the requirement of dual majorities, is discussed in chapter 3.)

Representation of employers' and employees' interests is entrusted to organizations under the sway of the political parties (see chapter 2). These organizations nominate the members of the carriers' boards, and thus political parties exercise a decisive influence on the management of the carriers. All social insurance carriers belong to the so-called Main Association of Social Insurance Carriers (*Hauptverband der Sozialversicherungstraeger*). The association represents the carriers' common interests to the government and the general public, and coordinates the carriers' international activities.

The third principle of the Austrian social insurance system dates from 1965: contributions and benefits are dynamic. In accordance with predetermined rules, contributions and benefits are regularly adjusted to bring them into line with current economic conditions as reflected in wage levels. For the sake of uniformity, the same method of rescaling benefits is also applied to social insurance schemes that cater to the self-employed, even though their actual income is determined by entirely different criteria. Although, broadly speaking, the criteria that determine the size of contributions are the same as those for benefits, increases in expenditures (for reasons that will be explained later) are not matched by a corresponding increase in contributions.

One final principle is worth noting. Insurance arises by operation of law in all occupations covered by compulsory insurance, irrespective of the worker's own wishes and inclinations. Although various forms of voluntary insurance exist, the number of persons using them is small and relatively insignificant. One person may be enrolled in several insurance schemes if he or she is engaged in more than one gainful occupation, each of which entails compulsory insurance (e.g., persons who work for more than one employer or who run their own businesses as well as working for an employer). Enrollment in different insurance schemes involves payment of more than one set of contributions; within limits it can correspondingly increase benefits.

Full and Part Insurance

Regardless of nationality, any person gainfully employed in Austria in an occupation covered by compulsory insurance is liable to such insurance from the day he or she starts work. There is no need for the person concerned to make any declaration of consent or even formally to enroll in the system—though registration with the relevant insurance carrier is required, failure to do so does not necessarily prevent coverage or the emergence of benefit claims. Thus in general terms, insurance vests in the work rather than in the individual worker.

For wage earners, farmers, and the self-employed in commerce and industry, insurance as a rule includes all three branches—health, industrial injury, and pension. In such cases it is customary to speak of *full insurance*, while instances in which a person is subject to compulsory insurance only in one or another branch are known as *partial insurance*. Even this apparent simplicity conceals complexity; for example, a pensioner is covered only by health insurance unless, of course, he or she is engaged in a gainful and insurable occupation; in such cases the pensioner is fully insured and is enrolled in the health insurance scheme *twice*, once as worker and once as a pensioner.

Only in pension insurance can a delay in registering an employee for insurance or tardiness in the payment of contributions result in a loss of benefits. But it is the employer, not the employee, on whom the law places the duty to register and to remit contributions. The relevant legal provisions are framed so as to minimize the danger of any such losses, and in special cases, retroactive payment of contributions is permitted if such payment will prevent the insured's being exposed to undue hardship.

Compulsory and Voluntary Insurance

Austrians look upon social insurance as an instrument devised to protect primarily blue- and white-collar workers, that is, persons who work for an employer. Such an attitude clearly does not leave much room for voluntary insurance. The extension of this protective system to farmers and the self-employed over the last few decades reflects a change in the fabric of society, a change that acceptance of the idea of social insurance as a means of protecting wage earners has almost imperceptibly brought about. Despite changes in general mores, however, the principle still holds that protection should be available only to persons who are gainfully occupied, and preferably to persons who have been gainfully occupied for some time.

In the 1970s this link between coverage and occupation lost some of its original strength as far as health insurance was concerned. As vast numbers of persons were compulsorily enrolled in social insurance, and thus eligible for health benefits, it was felt unreasonable to exclude the 3 percent of the population who were not subject to compulsory insurance from the protection of the statutory health insurance scheme. Thus in 1977 all residents of Austria, regardless of age or state of health, became eligible for voluntary participation in the national health insurance scheme.

Certain groups of people can also insure themselves voluntarily in the industrial injury insurance scheme, but voluntary participation in pension insurance still requires that the person concerned have been covered by compulsory insurance for specified minimum periods. A third form of voluntary insurance allows supplementary insurance for increased benefits in return for increased contributions. Available for pension and industrial injury insurance, it is restricted to persons already enrolled in those schemes.

Self-financing

Self-financing implies that the cost of benefits and their administration are financed from the contributions that the insured and their employers pay. Self-financing is fully practiced in health and industrial injury insurance for the employed, as well as in health insurance for the self-employed in commerce and industry and in pension insurance for notaries. All other forms of pension insurance, as well as health and industrial injury insurance for farmers, are financed in part from the public purse. The state's financial involvement is sometimes justified on the grounds that the state frequently requires insurance carriers to assume financial responsibility for tasks that can only with the greatest difficulty be described as falling within the scope of social insurance proper. In the case of pension schemes for the self-employed, the state, it is argued, merely acts the part of the (nonexistent) employer.

Benefits as Rights that Must Be Claimed

When an insured person fulfills both the general conditions for all benefits (e.g., the qualifying periods) and the conditions special to the benefit claimed (e.g., the attainment of pensionable age, sickness, pregnancy, etc.), he or she has a legal right to the level of benefit as determined by statute and by the bylaws of the appropriate insurance carrier. In these circumstances, the only formality required to obtain a benefit is to submit a demand for it. No benefit may be made available without a demand from the claimant (except in industrial injury insurance, where benefits may also be granted ex officio). A claimant's formal demand for a benefit is also required before an insurance carrier may deny an alleged obligation and thus open the way for court proceedings. As social insurance claims affect the claimant's standard of living very noticeably, the law has placed the ultimate decision about entitlement to and size of benefit in the hands of independent tribunals. A claimant dissatisfied with the ruling of a social insurance carrier appears before the tribunal as the plaintiff, the carrier as the defendant.

Insured Persons and Their Employers

The General Social Insurance Act has assigned to the term employed person a novel connotation, one that differs significantly from and in fact essentially transcends the meaning the term bears in the area of civil law. The relationship between master and servant in civil law is basically one of contract, pure and simple. But the ASVG bypasses the issue of contract by making the situation itself (a person works for another for pay and is personally and economically under the control of the employer) the pivotal point. This redefinition aims to prevent employers avoiding insurance liability by means of fictitious contracts. It also prevents situations in which one person, who to all intents and purposes is employed by another person, might be deprived of insurance coverage simply because no ostensible, legally effective employment contract exists to regulate the relationship between them. True, it is not always easy to decide in a given case whether a particular person is working "personally and economically" under the control of another. Certain indicators, however, point in that direction: for example, the absence of discretionary powers regarding the way in which the work is to be performed; the requirement to obey the other person's instructions and directions; the need to stick to certain hours of work; the obligation to perform the work in person; and the ownership of tools and other equipment needed for the job not by the worker but by the person for whom he or she works. The period of employment must also exceed a few hours in duration. The motives that prompt a person to take up work are, on the other hand, of no relevance to the question of insurance liability.

Yet the matter of who constitutes an employed person is not clearcut. Despite a host of court decisions over the last few decades, the question has time and again given rise to serious difficulties of interpretation and, in their wake, to legal disputes. If the matter is doubtful, the authorities, as well as the courts, tend to affirm rather than deny the existence of insurance liability.

The ASVG definition points to the two principal classes of insured persons, namely blue- and white-collar workers. The distinction is relevant in the area of pension insurance, where each class has its own pension insurance carrier; it also affects the size of contributions payable by the employed and their employers.

To round off the picture, mention must also be made of miners, for whom a separate insurance carrier has been established. The term *miners* here means persons who are employed as blue- or white-collar workers in businesses engaged in the production of salt and minerals (coal, ores, and limestone) other than petroleum.

The ASVG has also redefined the term employer in a manner that transcends the word's meaning in civil law. The act holds a person on whose account any activities involving the employment of another person are pursued to be an employer within the meaning of the act; it makes no difference whether the employed person receives remuneration from the employer or from a third party (e.g., a waiter is employed by a restaurant owner even if receiving money from the restaurant's clients in the form of tips). On the other hand, the mere fact that a person pays wages does not automatically confer the status of employer, because he or she may pay them on behalf of someone else.

Employership involves the duty to register employed persons with the appropriate insurance carrier and to give the carrier all the information it needs. Employers are also obliged to remit to the carriers both the employer's contribution and the employees' contributions, which are deducted from pay.

Dependents

Insurance extends to the dependents of the insured person. In all three branches of insurance the term *dependents* covers the employed person's spouse and children. That somewhat narrow definition has, however, been widened in some sorts of insurance and also in respect of some benefits, partly by statute and partly by bylaw of the carriers.

For a person to be recognized as the spouse of an insured person, the marriage between that person and the insured must have been solemnized in the eyes of Austrian law and must not have been terminated by annulment, divorce, or the death of the insured. Persons insured in their own right have no claim as dependents on their spouses' health insurance. If marriage with an insured person is terminated for reasons other than the death of the insured, the noninsured person's right to the insurance coverage of the insured spouse ceases on the date when the judgment that terminated the marriage enters into legal effect. But anyone may join the statutory health insurance scheme on a voluntary basis, and if a divorced spouse does so within six weeks of the end of the marriage, the award of health benefits will not depend upon the completion of a qualifying period.

Since June 1, 1981, widows and widowers have been treated according to the principle of equality. The death of the insured gives rise to death benefits, available to a surviving spouse under the terms of the pension insurance scheme, provided that the marriage was still valid when the insured spouse died. If death was a result of an industrial accident or disease, the surviving spouse is entitled to claim not only benefit under the pension insurance scheme but also the death benefit available under the industrial injury insurance scheme.

The spouse of an earlier, terminated marriage may also be entitled to death benefits under the terms of the pension and industrial injury insurance schemes, provided that the insured was at the time of death legally obliged to contribute to the spouse's maintenance. But the death benefit is due the former spouse only if his or her right to claim maintenance from the insured was based on a judicial decision, an agreement made in court, or a contractual arrangement that the spouses had concluded before their marriage was terminated. The amount of death benefit that may be paid to a former spouse may not exceed what is owing to the surviving spouse, nor may it be more than the amount of regular maintenance that the insured paid while alive. The award of a survivor's pension automatically enrolls the recipient in the statutory health insurance scheme.

The term *children* is construed more or less similarly in all three branches of insurance. It refers to legitimate, illegitimate, legitimated, and adopted children from their birth until their eighteenth birthday. As a rule, childhood ends at the age of eighteen; the status of childhood may, however, be extended beyond that age in cases where the child receives full-time instruction or occupational training or stands in need of special protection. In the first case childhood may be extended until the age of twenty-six, further if completion of studies or training has been delayed on account of military service or some other unavoidable obstacle. The second case refers to people who are incapable of work as a result either of a disease or the loss of physical or mental faculty that they contracted or sustained at a time when they were or were deemed to be children. In such cases, the status of childhood can be extended *sine die* to last until the capacity for work ceases. In order to provide a measure of financial relief to parents, the status of childhood as far as health insurance is concerned extends after full-time instruction or training ends. The extra coverage lasts until the person concerned takes up a paid job that involves enrollment in social insurance, to a maximum of one year.

Social Insurance Carriers

The administration of social insurance is entrusted to the carriers. Their organization is determined by statute, and insofar as they discharge statutorily defined duties of a kind normally performed by the government, they assume the character of public authorities. They do not, however, lose their corporate status, which enables them to own property or to sue or be sued in their own name.

The legal nature of the carriers, and particularly the place they occupy in the Austrian system of constitutional and administrative law, is a complex matter. As pointed out earlier, the carriers owe their existence and the manner of their organization to statutory law, which more than anything else places them outside the realm of private law. And yet they are certainly not integrated into the government bureaucracy, nor are they even affiliated with the bureaucracy. Nevertheless, some of the functions that they are called upon to discharge are undeniably of a typical governmental character. When the carriers discharge such functions (e.g., when they rule on a person's insurance liability), they are acting the part of public authorities and assume such a character. This state of affairs implies, among other things, that in common with public authorities the carriers' finances and business management are subject to the scrutiny of the General Accounting Office, that their officers must not divulge information that they attain in the course of their duties to any unauthorized person, and so forth. However, when the carriers act in a distinctly nongovernmental matter (e.g., when they fix the salaries of their staff), they enjoy a large measure of autonomy, and the restrictions on public authorities do not apply to them.

Those social insurance carriers that administer health insurance for employed persons (other than miners or railway employees) are traditionally known as sickness funds (*Krankenkassen*). There are nineteen of these funds; nine are organized on a strictly territorial basis, one for each province, while the other ten are associated with specific industrial and commercial sectors.

Two carriers, the Austrian Railways Insurance Carrier and the Social Insurance Carrier for Farmers, handle all three branches of insurance. The others are competent only in one or another branch, and pension insurance is administered by no fewer than seven different carriers.

The General Accident Insurance Carrier is concerned with industrial injury insurance for employed persons other than railway employees and for self-employed persons in commerce and industry. For wage earners (other than miners and railway workers), there are two separate pension insurance carriers, one catering to blue-collar and the other to white-collar workers. The Austrian Miners Insurance Carrier is responsible for health and pension insurance in that industry. The Social Insurance Carrier for Self-employed Persons in Commerce and Industry administers health and pension insurance; the Civil Servants Insurance Carrier handles industrial injury and health insurance for those in government service; and the Insurance Carrier for Austrian Notaries is responsible for operating that profession's pension scheme (see table 5.1).

All twenty-eight social insurance carriers are federated into the Main Association of Austrian Social Insurance Carriers, which, broadly speaking, acts on behalf of the constituent organizations in all matters affecting their common interests. It is, for instance, the main association that negotiates with the Austrian medical association (in Austrian terms, the Central Chamber of Physicians) the fees that medical practitioners under contract to the health insurance carriers receive for their services. The main association is also involved in the negotiation of social security agreements with other countries.

Contribution Assessment Basis and Rates

Contributions are in principle related to earnings, in the sense that their size is determined with reference to the gross amount earned in a contribution period. But the whole of earnings are not necessarily taken into account for assessment purposes. In all three branches of insurance contributions are payable only on that part of a person's earnings which is

TABLE 5.1

Austrian Social Insurance Carriers

Insurance Scheme	Carriers
Industrial Injuries	General Accident Insurance Carrier
	Austrian Railways Insurance Carrier
	Social Insurance Carrier for Farmers
	Civil Servants Insurance Carrier
Health	9 Regional Sickness Funds
	10 Enterprise Sickness Funds
	Austrian Miners Industry Insurance Carrier
	Social Insurance Carrier for Self-Employed Persons in Commerce and Industry
	Austrian Railways Insurance Carrier
	Social Insurance Carrier for Farmers
	Civil Servants Insurance Carrier
Pension	Pension Insurance Carrier for Blue-Collar Workers
	Pension Insurance Carrier for White-Collar Workers
	Austrian Miners Insurance Carrier
	Social Insurance Carrier for Self-Employed Persons in Commerce and Industry
	Austrian Railways Insurance Carrier
	Social Insurance Carrier for Farmers
	Insurance Carrier for Austrian Notaries

below a statutorily defined maximum—the *contribution ceiling* or *maximum assessment basis*. Earnings above that ceiling are disregarded for contribution purposes; that part of earnings on which contributions are payable is called the *contribution assessment basis*. Contribution ceilings are raised year by year so that the proportion of a person's earnings on which contributions are payable increases in step with wages and salaries. In 1985 the contribution ceiling was S20,400 (20,400 schillings) a month for health insurance and S24,600 for industrial injury and pension insurance. Only some 15 percent of the total Austrian work force have earnings that exceed the ceiling for industrial injury and pension insurance.

The law also lays down a minimum amount—a *contribution floor* —on which contributions can be assessed and levied, irrespective of actual earnings. Such minimums, however, have little meaning in practical terms.

The term *contribution period* denotes the period of time for which contributions are payable. The length of the period is determined by the length of the pay period; it is normally equal to one week in the case of blue-collar workers, if, as is customary in Austria, they are paid weekly; in the case of white-collar workers, who are traditionally paid at monthly intervals, the contribution period is equal to one calendar

TABLE 5.2
Contribution Rates, 1985

Type of Insurance	Total Rate	Employee Contribution	Employer Contribution
Blue-collar workers*			
Health	6.3%	3.15%	3.15%
Industrial injury	1.5	—	1.5
Pension	18.5	9.25	9.25
Add'l charge to pension	4.2	1.0	3.2
Miners' pension	23.0	8.75	14.25
White-collar workers			
Health	5.0	2.5	2.5
Industrial injury	1.5	—	1.5
Pension	18.5	9.25	9.25
Add'l charge to pension	4.2	1.0	3.2
Miners' pension	23.0	8.75	14.25

Note: *These rates are applicable in cases where a blue-collar worker is covered by the Continued Payment of Wages Act of 1974. This act makes provision for unabated payment by the employer of wages due to a blue-collar worker for at least four weeks should the worker, on account of illness, become incapable of work, provided that the employment in question is covered by the act. An employer, on producing the appropriate medical certificate, can reclaim from the health insurance carrier concerned the amount of wages he or she paid the worker during the period of sickness; the owners of smaller establishments can even claim from the carrier a lump sum to reimburse their expenses for such ancillary wage costs as social insurance contributions. The scheme is financed in part (2.6%) by contributions that all employers are required to pay into a special fund, which is administered by the health insurance carriers. Legally the employers' contributions represent premiums payable to a compulsory insurance scheme through which employers insure against a specific form of liability to their blue-collar workers. As long as a worker draws pay under the act, he or she is precluded from receiving cash benefits under the terms of the health insurance scheme. Indeed, when the act came into force, the health insurance rates for blue-collar workers covered by the act were lowered. (White-collar workers are in the case of illness entitled to full pay for at least six weeks, followed by up to four more weeks of half pay. The costs involved are borne by the employers.)

Blue-collar workers not covered by the act are subject to different contribution rates for health insurance: Uncovered workers in 1985 contributed 3.15% and their employers contributed 3.15%, for a total of 6.3%.

TABLE 5.3

Maximum Monthly Insurance Contributions, 1985 (in Schillings)

	Total	Employee Contribution	Employer Contribution
Blue-collar workers			
Health	1,285.20	642.60	642.60
Industrial injury	369.00	—	369.00
Pension	4,551.00	2,275.50	2,275.50
Add'l charge to pension	1,033.20	246.00	787.20
White-collar workers			
Health	1,020.00	510.00	510.00
Industrial injury	369.00	—	369.00
Pension	4,551.00	2,275.50	2,275.50
Add'l charge to pension	1,033.20	246.00	787.20

month (the latter, regardless of its actual length, is taken to be thirty days).

The actual contribution payable in each individual case is computed by applying to the contribution assessment basis the contribution rate appropriate to the branch of insurance and to the class of insured persons concerned. Contribution rates are expressed in percentages and are fixed by law (those for 1985 appear in table 5.2). It is generally agreed that it would be unwise to exceed the current levels of contributions in the present economic conditions. To try to balance receipts and expenditures in the face of rising costs, particularly in health insurance, cost-reducing measures were taken in 1981, when the charges that insured persons pay toward the costs of such items as drugs, dentures, and spectacles were increased. Further alterations were made in pension insurance in 1985 to counteract a substantial rise in expenditures.

Taking into account both the contribution rates and the contribution ceilings, the maximum amounts for contributions payable in 1985 were as shown in table 5.3.

Denial of Benefit

A claimant who satisfies the statutory conditions appropriate to a specific benefit will not invariably receive that benefit. There are instances when it may be denied, either permanently or for a finite period of time. In some cases the law extinguishes a claim to benefit altogether; for example, when the injury giving rise to the claim was self-inflicted, and when the basis for a claim is a criminal act by the insured that results in more than one year in jail.

Sometimes forfeiture of benefit is not mandatory but lies within the discretion of the insurance carrier. In such cases forfeiture depends upon the insured person's having received a previous warning from the carrier. The warning advises the insured that persistent failure to comply with one or more of the carrier's instructions, usually in the field of medical care (e.g., the invitation to undergo medical treatment, to submit to a checkup, or to participate in rehabilitation), will ultimately result in the loss of rights to benefits or to a pension under the industrial injury or pension insurance schemes.

There are also instances where the right to benefit is neither extinguished nor forfeited, but where payment is suspended either in whole or in part. The purpose of such suspensions is not to penalize the insured for misconduct but either to avoid the duplication of benefit or to prevent the continued payment of benefit no longer needed. Classical examples in this respect include persons receiving a pension or health benefits and, simultaneously, earnings from gainful employment, and persons drawing disability pension while receiving in-patient treatment in a hospital. (It may be necessary to point out that retirement from work is one of the conditions for the award of pension, and thus the law partially suspends payment of a pension if the pensioner resumes gainful employment. The extent of suspension depends on the size of the pension and of the earnings.)

Insurance Eligibility, Voluntary Insurance, and Enrollment in Insurance

Austrian social insurance law is in principle territorial: it applies to all persons, regardless of their nationality, whose place of employment is located within Austria. Several exceptions to this general rule recognize the uncertain territorial status of those who work for a firm based in Austria but travel elsewhere, for Austrian social insurance law continues to apply even if the "place of employment" is temporarily outside Austria. Similarly, a person employed by a business in Austria that sends him or her abroad to work continues to be eligible for Austrian social insurance for a maximum of two years.

All employed persons (blue- and white-collar, miners and apprentices) and various other groups that the law includes as employed persons (e.g., workmen employed in their own homes who own their own tools, artists, musicians, railway porters, tourist guides) are covered by compulsory, full-scale insurance. However, the law exempts some classes of the employed from the general rule that any kind of gainful employment should entail full-scale insurance. As a result, exempted persons are only insured in one or two of the three branches of social insurance; for example, civil servants, who have their own pension scheme, are enrolled only in the health and occupational injury branches of social insurance.

Compulsory insurance starts as soon as a person enters a gainful occupation of a kind that gives rise to such coverage. The start of voluntary insurance is, of course, determined by the person who wishes to pay voluntary contributions. The business of enrolling the insured in the social security system is entrusted to the regional sickness funds. Although primarily responsible for the administration of health insurance in their respective areas, the funds also collect contributions payable under the unemployment, industrial injury, and pension insurance schemes.

The rule, mentioned earlier, that certain facts and circumstances give rise to compulsory insurance in themselves and by operation of law implies that coverage is not conditional on the employed person's being registered with a regional sickness fund for insurance purposes, either by the employer or by someone acting on the employer's behalf. Nevertheless, for administrative reasons, the fund needs timely notice of all facts and circumstances that have a bearing upon the relationship between fund and insured. Upon entry into insurance coverage the insured is assigned an insurance number that shows in code sex and date of birth. (These numbers are issued by the Main Association of Austrian Social Insurance Carriers.) All further data relating to the insured are, if important for social insurance purposes, filed under the person's insurance number. Both the engagement of staff for and their subsequent discharge from insurable employment, as well as any change in employment conditions relevant to social insurance, such as a change in pay rate, must be reported by the employer to the local regional sickness fund within three days. The employer's duty in the matter of reporting devolves upon the employee if the employer enjoys diplomatic status or has no place of business inside Austria. The employer's duty to furnish information to the fund is matched by the fund's right to check the information and to arrange examinations, inquiries, and inspections by its own officials. Any information thus gained must be kept confidential. Failure to submit the requisite reports to the fund constitutes an administrative offense, which in the interests of proper and smooth administration may be punished by fines and in serious cases by imprisonment.

Financing Insurance Schemes

Calculation of Contributions

Eligibility for insurance coverage involves the responsibility to pay contributions. The benefits provided by social insurance, together with the costs of administration, are paid for partly by insured persons' contributions and, where appropriate, partly by the contributions of their employers. A contribution from public funds is available for the pension insurance schemes as well as for the health and industrial injury insurance schemes for farmers.

A basis for calculating the size of contributions (the contribution assessment basis) requires a quantity that cannot easily be manipulated and that arises exclusively from or in connection with the insurable employment concerned. The ASVG has made the insured person's earnings the relevant quantity. *Earnings* as employed in the act includes any remuneration whether in cash or in kind, to which the insured is entitled by virtue of insurable activity and all job-related income the insured receives from his or her employer or from a third party (e.g., tips).

Austrian custom, the reader will recall, is to pay employed persons as if they were employed fourteen months each calendar year. A special bonus, equal in amount to one month's pay, is given at Christmas and in July, at the beginning of the vacation season. In legal parlance these extra paychecks are known as "special payments," and they are taken into account for contribution purposes to the extent to which the aggregate in a calendar year does not exceed twice the monthly contribution ceiling. The rates at which contributions were levied and the maximum amounts payable in 1985 appear in tables 5.2 and 5.3.

Collection of Contributions

In principle the calculation and remittance of contributions are duties that the law assigns to employers. They must pay both their own contributions and their employees' deductibles for each contribution period. Payment must be made before a prescribed period of time expires, and failure to comply may result in the imposition of a variety of penalties. In practice, however, to facilitate matters for owners of small businesses, the local regional sickness fund informs employers of the amount they are supposed to remit for coverage of their staff. In the case of large or medium-size undertakings the regional sickness fund is content to receive lists of wages and salaries due to each employee. The accuracy of these lists is open to future examination and inspection by the fund's auditors.

Contributions are payable on the last day of the contribution period; after an eleven-day grace period interest is charged on any outstanding amount. The federal minister for social affairs adjusts this interest rate from time to time to bring it into line with current interest levels.

Automatic Nature of Contributions

Because Austrian social security is dynamic, both benefits and contributions are adjusted to reflect current economic trends without requiring a special act of Parliament.

When Parliament considered the General Social Insurance Act in 1955, the problem of maintaining the intrinsic value of cash benefits proved to be intractable. But this gap in the law did not become apparent before the mid-1960s, for previously the inflation rate was insignificant and the purchasing power of the schilling exceptionally stable. Only in the wake of the expansion of the Austrian economy and the significant rise in the wage level did the question of whether and in what form pensioners should be allowed to share in the general increase in the national wealth begin to gain importance. The Austrian People's party inclined to the view that cash benefits should be brought into line with current economic conditions by adjustments indexed to certain economic indicators, but with Parliament through legislation having a say on the extent of adjustment on each occasion. The Socialists, however, advocated a system that would automatically secure the intrinsic value of benefits without intervention by Parliament (or any other agency) by strictly linking benefits to economic indicators. They held that benefits should be revalued year by year—a trend other than an upward trend was inconceivable—and that the extent of revaluation should be calculated each year according to a formula determined in advance by legislation. There were only two points on which the two political parties were in full agreement: first, to adjust benefits to current economic conditions required a parallel adjustment of contributions, and second, the problem involved more than the preservation of the intrinsic value of benefits.

The problem arose at the time of the Great Coalition between the two major parties, and so a compromise had to be reached. The two parties eventually agreed on and Parliament then adopted a combination of the two proposed systems. This "dynamic" solution used a predetermined formula to adjust benefits to current economic trends without special legislation each time; but adjustment was not to be automatic. It would require concerted action by the federal minister for social affairs and the Main Committee of Parliament, who could thus provide for adjustments that did not necessarily conform with the economic indicators. Still working more than twenty years since the arrangement first went into operation, the outcome of the long negotiations between the political parties has stood the test of time.

This discussion of how social insurance is financed is confined to a consideration of the rules that determine how contributions adjust to the changing conditions of the Austrian economy. The earnings of persons who are still working provide the starting point for adjustments. In Austria it is customary for the trade unions to put forward wage claims in roughly annual intervals, so negotiations between the two sides of industry take place once a year. The trade unions as a rule will demand that both the minimum rates as laid down in collective agreements and the rates actually paid should increase by a certain percentage. Negotiations usually result in wages and salaries being increased by slightly more than the rate of inflation, so that there is a slight increase in real disposable income for employees. The general level of earnings has thus gone up steadily over the years. At the same time the yield from insurance contributions, because it is related to earnings, has gone up automatically. But there are also other quantities (e.g., maximum and minimum assessment bases) that need current adjustment. To effect such adjustments, the federal minister for social affairs establishes each year the increase in the size of the average contribution assessment basis on two appointed days, one in January and one in July.

In this way the minister establishes a special wage index, called the *revaluation coefficient*. In order to keep as closely in step as possible with the development of the economy, this coefficient, say for the year

1986, is determined by contrasting the average contribution assessment basis arising from the counts in January 1983, July 1983, and January 1984 with the average contribution assessment basis arising from the counts in January 1984, July 1984, and January 1985. Having in this manner established the revaluation coefficient for 1986, all quantities that bear on the size of contributions are multiplied by the coefficient without further action by any legislative or administrative body. Thus in contradistinction to benefits, which are adjusted dynamically in the sense explained above, contributions and maximum and minimum contribution assessment bases are varied—in practice, raised—automatically.

State Spending on Social Insurance

As with most other social security systems, in Austria state financial support to social insurance schemes is of the greatest importance to their functioning. All pension insurance schemes (except that for notaries), as well as the health and industrial injury insurance schemes for farmers, receive financial assistance from the state; the reason behind state aid for pension insurance schemes is that the size of a pension takes account not only of contribution periods when contributions were actually paid but also of periods when the insured, for reasons beyond his or her control, was unable to pay contributions. The latter is known as an *equivalent period,* and the most important such periods are times of school attendance (within limits), war service and captivity, the first twelve months after the birth of each child for mothers, and times when sickness or unemployment benefits were paid to the insured (also within limits). An equivalent period of a special kind was occasioned by the fact that old age pension insurance for blue-collar workers only came into effect beginning January 1, 1939. For blue-collar workers, therefore, periods of employment completed before that date rank, at least in part, as equivalent periods.

Equivalent periods obviously increase the length of most insurance records and thereby the rate of pension benefit for a large number of claimants, which in turn involves the insurance carriers concerned in additional financial liabilities that are not matched by additional contributions. These circumstances make it appear only fair that the state, which places new burdens on the carriers by passing laws, should grant the carriers some measure of financial relief.

As a result of economic developments and ever-increasing automation in industry, the number of white-collar workers is growing faster than the number of blue-collar workers, and many blue-collar workers are moving into posts carrying white-collar status. This process has changed the ratio between blue-collar workers still working and those receiving pensions; a similar process can be observed in the cases of self-employed persons in commerce and industry, and especially farmers. These circumstances justify the financial assistance that the state makes available in all pension insurance schemes and in health and industrial injury insurance for farmers, on the grounds that such assistance is needed to smooth out the effects of macroeconomic and structural change (see table 5.4).

Social insurance as an institution is also used deliberately to redistribute income within society. Ceilings on contributions and benefits admittedly tend to lessen the redistributive effect, since earnings above the ceilings (and thus beyond the maximum assessment basis) are not taken into account for contribution purposes. Nevertheless, earnings above the ceiling are subject to income tax. As state financial assistance to the various social insurance schemes obviously comes out of general taxation, the state in effect induces some measure of income redistribution even with regard to earnings exempted from social insurance contributions.

The size of the federal contribution and the manner of its computation vary from one social insurance scheme to another. In health insurance for farmers, the state matches each contribution paid by the insured on a one-to-one basis. In industrial injury insurance for farmers, the state pays a sum equal to one-third of aggregate contributions by the insured as a federal contribution. In all three pension insurance

TABLE 5.4

Number of Pensions Paid

for Every Thousand Workers, 1979 and 1984

Pension Insurance Scheme	1979	1984
General Social Insurance Act	479	538
Blue-collar workers and miners	619	696
White-collar workers	293	350
Self-employed (Commerce and Industry) Act	768	747
Farmers' Social Insurance Act	919	953

TABLE 5.5
State Contributions
to Social Insurance, 1984

Insurance Scheme	State Assistance (millions of schillings)	State Assistance (as % of federal budget)
Health, industrial injury, farmers' pension	9,000	65.0%
Pension: self-employed	8,250	68.9
Pension: wage earners	23,600	20.2
Total	40,850	28.7

schemes (for wage earners, farmers, and the self-employed) the state is obliged to indemnify the carriers against any loss they may sustain in operating the schemes in question. Under the provisions of the ASVG the state is obliged to refund to pension insurance carriers the amount by which their disbursements exceed their receipts plus a sum equal to 0.5 percent of disbursements, a procedure intended to help carriers set up reserve funds. A similar procedure is applicable to pension schemes for the self-employed but subject to the modification that before an excess of disbursements over receipts (and thereby the state's liability to make good any deficit) is established, the state must pay in a sum equal to the aggregate amount of contributions by those insured under the scheme. In a sense the state plays the part of the employer.

The state rendered substantial financial assistance to the various social insurance carriers in 1984, as table 5.5 shows.

HEALTH INSURANCE

Health insurance is designed to improve the physical and mental health of the insured and their dependents; to prevent, diagnose, and adequately treat illness; to provide payments to individuals incapable of working during a limited period of illness; and to meet special needs arising from the confinement of women and the burial of the insured and their dependents.

Only in the 1960s did preventive medicine start to be recognized as one of the tasks that health insurance should tackle. The general public's increased interest in medical and social measures for preventing illness, prophylaxis, and rehabilitation probably arose from their feeling that traditional public health policy regarding both diagnosis and therapy was no longer adequate to provide comprehensive protection of the public health.

These newly realized needs found expression in the 1972 establishment of a special government department, the Federal Ministry of Health and Environmental Protection, to concern itself specifically with public health and related matters. Nevertheless, compulsory health insurance, always regarded as the most effective tool of public health policy, remains the responsibility of the Federal Ministry of Social Affairs. The paramount importance of health insurance in the area of public health is underlined by a constitutional peculiarity: in the field of institutional health care, the federal Parliament is limited to enacting general rules and adumbrating broad principles; all details, such as the provision and management of hospitals, are matters to be settled by the parliaments and governments of each of the nine provinces. To bring out the full importance of health insurance and to appreciate the position it occupies in the Austrian social security system, it is necessary to cast a brief glance at the principles that underlie the Austrian health system and the policy that finds expression in the system.

Public health policy, or at least its modest beginnings, can be identified as far back as the eighteenth century. Austria's present-day public health system is still organized along lines determined by laws passed a century ago. Moreover, the current division of executive powers between the federal government and the various provincial governments is now more than sixty years old.

Attempts to modernize the organization of institutional health care have not been lacking, but all have foundered on this federal-provincial division of powers. Enshrined in the Austrian Constitution, this division can be abolished or modified only with the consent of both major parties. The reason is that constitutional law is entrenched and can be amended or repealed only if two-thirds of the lower chamber (*Nationelrat*) of the federal Parliament agrees. Neither political party has ever commanded such a majority, and neither is ever likely to. Since 1970 the Socialist Party has held a majority at the federal level while the People's party has controlled six of the nine provincial parliaments. A constitutional amendment to transfer executive power over public health matters to the federal authorities would therefore weaken the People's party, which is why no joint legislative action has been taken. Moreover, public health matters and, in particular, the provision and running of hospitals are of considerable financial significance, which aggravates the political situation. Most hospitals are administered by local (municipal and provincial) authorities, and, constitutionally, financial responsibility is also theirs. This responsibility involves them in financial difficulties that are serious and getting worse.

As about 97 percent of the population are covered by the statutory health insurance scheme and must therefore be accommodated in hospitals in case of need, the fees paid by the sickness funds on behalf of inpatients form the principal source of income for these hospitals. These fees, however, cover only a fraction of actual costs of medical attention, surgical treatment, drugs, dressings, and room and board. Added to these fees are contributions that the federal government pays (though it is under no constitutional obligation to do so). The balance between receipts and expenditures must be paid for by hospital owners—the municipality or the province concerned. The modest extent to which the sickness funds contribute toward hospital outlays (no more than 50 to 60 percent of actual costs) explains why, in comparison to other European countries, government health insurance in Austria is on the low side.

In an atmosphere of tension and among mutually exclusive interests, the federal minister for health attempts to pursue policy adequate to preserve the health of individuals through early diagnosis of disease and to lower infant mortality and morbidity while providing greater protection of expectant and nursing mothers. Austria's mortality rate is around 13 per thousand, rather high by European standards and likely to stay high for the next decade or so. The reason lies in the age distribution of the Austrian population, in turn mainly the consequence of two world wars (see table 6.1). As elsewhere, there is a marked preponderance of women among the elderly. In comparison with international standards, infant mortality is still very high, although attempts to lower it have met with some success.

Great efforts are needed to improve housing conditions and hygiene and medical care at workplaces. Recent advances in the field of occupational health are designed to reduce disease and accidents in factories and workshops. The law makes it incumbent upon employers to provide such services; they may, however, discharge their duties by paying the appropriate fees in order to use the services of the occupational medicine centers owned by the General Accident Insurance Carrier.

Health care and health education are accorded special importance. A health program elaborated over the last few years is intended to take care of the entire population from cradle to grave. Special maternity grants have been introduced, payment being contingent upon mothers submitting their babies to specified medical examinations in the first two years of life. Children from the age of six are in the care of the school health service, and of course employment or apprenticeship involves automatic enrollment in compulsory health insurance. Juveniles are urged to undergo medical examinations to monitor their general health and ascertain their fitness for particular careers. All these medical services and tests are devised by the Main Association of Austrian Social Insurance Carriers in conjunction with the medical profession and the Federal Health Ministry. Annual checkups are provided free of charge for all adults, regardless of age, sex, or nationality. Performed in out-patient clinics operating under the auspices of the sickness funds or in hospitals, as well as in doctors' offices, they are paid for from the public purse except where the examinee is covered by a statutory health insurance scheme, in which case the carrier pays for the checkup.

Yet all attempts to interest the population in annual checkups have met with little response, although doctors agree that annual checkups are the most effective means of preventing ill health. Bureaucratic requirements may act as a deterrent in some instances. That an overwhelming proportion of the population is covered by statutory insurance and can demand an examination at any time may also account for the public's lack of enthusiasm for state-sponsored schemes for preventive checkups.

Various medical services are available under the Austrian health system. As the patient's first line of defense in case of illness, the general practitioner is at the center of the system; no less important are specialists and the out-patient clinics of the sickness funds and the hospitals. At the end of 1981, 18,888 members of the medical profession, of whom approximately 4,500 were undergoing postgraduate training, were practicing in Austria—about 250 doctors to every 100,000 inhabitants. Thus in comparison with most European countries Austria is well supplied with doctors. It is, however, worth noting that in recent years the proportion of general practitioners has conspicuously decreased and the number of specialists has risen. General practitioners tend to complain that their work load is excessive, but more than half of them have undertaken additional employment in out-patient clinics or the public health service as extra sources of income. Because they are overworked and (at least in their view) underpaid by the sickness funds, doctors tend to have their patients admitted to hospitals even in cases when on strictly medical grounds hospitalization is not absolutely necessary or even desirable. As a result, despite the comparatively large number of hospital beds in Austria, 11 for every 1,000 inhabitants, hospitals are overcrowded, and expensively equipped acute-care wards are used to accommodate long-term patients who do not need acute care. The age structure of the population tends to aggravate this situation further. Promising efforts to improve the care of the elderly, such as meals-on-wheels and home nursing, have been started, but no statistics regarding their effectiveness are yet available.

Regional disparities in the distribution of doctors practicing as self-employed persons present problems of a special kind. The number of doctors with practices in urban areas is unduly high, while rural districts and the suburbs tend to be underserved. Although the regional sickness funds cannot instruct doctors on where to open practices, they have ways, in conjunction with local authorities, to help establish surgeries in underserved areas. Particularly important is the agreement between the Main Association of Austrian Social Insurance Carriers and the Austrian medical association (the Central Chamber of Physicians), which fixes the number and location of practices for social insurance purposes in a manner clearly designed to lure doctors to underserved areas.

Efforts to improve the national health have intensified tremendously since 1970. Social insurance has excellent facilities of its own (outpatient clinics, hospitals, rehabilitation centers, convalescent homes) and formidable financial resources to use in the political tug-of-war about public health. Social insurance is thus at the very heart of these efforts. Mother and child care, medical inspections of juveniles and adults, vaccination campaigns, and medical and social rehabilitation are the principal outcomes of these efforts. But in individual health care general practitioners and specialists clearly dominate, at least in sheer numbers, over institutions. Nevertheless, the social insurance carriers largely determine the extent of services provided by the medical profession as a whole, because they, in conjunction with the medical association, set fees and heavily influence the number and location of practices.

The ASVG requires that the relationship between self-employed doctors and regional sickness funds be a contractual one for all health insurance schemes, and as such subject to the provisions of private law. A comprehensive agreement between the medical association and the

Main Association of Austrian Social Insurance Carriers settles all relevant points in the relationship—number and location of practices, mutual rights and duties, manner of selection of doctors, and above all remuneration. The terms of the agreement become automatically and by law an integral part of contractual arrangements between individual doctors and regional sickness funds. These are terms that represent compulsory law; the funds may not deviate from them in their arrangements with individual doctors.

Contingencies to Be Met by Health Insurance

The event that gives rise to benefit, or the peril insured against, is known by the general term *contingency*. In the present context the contingency in question is illness, which the law defines as a "pathological physical or mental condition that necessitates medical treatment." Medical treatment is treatment intended as far as possible to restore, strengthen, or improve a person's state of health, capacity for work, and ability to attend to his or her own personal and basic needs. Treatment must be adequate but not exceed what is considered clinically necessary. Hence the regional sickness funds are not obliged to provide, for example, cosmetic surgery unless the disfigurement concerned militates against the insured person's professional career. On the other hand, all measures to remove an organ for transplant are regarded as taken to meet the contingency of illness, and the regional sickness funds must take financial responsibility for them. Medical treatment that health insurance is required to provide consists of three main categories: medical attendance; the supply of drugs; and the supply of medical appliances. Travel expenses are also borne by the regional sickness funds.

To benefit from the services of a medical practitioner, the insured must obtain from his or her employer a so-called sickness voucher, which proves that the individual is insured and that the regional sickness fund that issued the voucher will cover the cost of treatment. The voucher also serves as the basis for the doctor's remuneration by the fund. Special vouchers are available for dental work and medical specialists' services. As a rule, the insured can obtain specialist treatment only by being referred by a general practitioner; however, the patient may go directly to a specialist in certain branches of medicine.

The insured is free to choose a doctor and may even choose one who is not under contract to the appropriate regional sickness fund. In such cases, however, the fund will reimburse only the amount it would have paid to a doctor under contract. Usually a patient will visit a contract doctor, or an out-patient clinic of the regional sickness fund or a hospital under contract to the fund. Across Austria some 75 percent of all general practitioners and 60 percent of all specialists are under contract to one or more regional sickness funds.

If the patient is insured under the ASVG, general practitioners' and specialists' services are free of charge to the patient; in the case of health insurance schemes for self-employed persons, the patient will as a rule be required to bear 20 percent of the cost of treatment. Doctors providing treatment at the expense of the regional sickness funds have complete clinical discretion regardless of the expense of treatment and therapy.

For economy's sake doctors may in principle prescribe at the expense of the regional sickness funds only those drugs included on a list compiled by the Main Association of Austrian Social Insurance Carriers. The drugs specified on the list are supplied by retail pharmacies on the basis of doctors' prescriptions and are paid for by the regional sickness funds, but a nominal charge is made for each prescription filled. Payable by the insured, this charge may be waived on the grounds of low income.

Austrian pharmacies may supply approximately 6,200 drugs. More than 2,800 appear on the main association's approved list. So, for all intents and purposes, doctors enjoy complete freedom in the matter of prescriptions, especially as 75 percent of all prescriptions involve no more than about 200 drugs. In cases of special need, drugs absent from the approved list may nevertheless be prescribed.

Because of the large numbers covered by health insurance there is virtually no market in Austria for drugs not approved by the main association. It is therefore a matter of the greatest importance to pharmaceutical companies to get their products approved. New products are referred to a commission on which social insurance carriers, pharmacists, and pharmacologists are represented. Manufacturers are entitled to be heard by the commission before it makes its decisions. If two drugs of equal effectiveness are submitted, preference will as a rule be given to the cheaper product, a practice that obviously tends to surpress price levels and is of great importance in Austria, which has no sizable pharmaceutical industry of its own.

Austrians use the term *medical appliance* to mean spectacles, arch supports, and trusses, as well as artificial limbs and eyes. Broadly speaking, these appliances are supplied at the expense of the regional sickness fund concerned. However, the insured must bear a portion of the costs, and the fund's contribution toward the price of the article may not exceed maximum amounts that are fixed year by year in the fund's bylaws. In cases warranting special consideration (financial distress of the insured or other pressing circumstances), the patient's deductible is waived.

Regional sickness funds are obliged to provide insured persons with dental service. Dental treatment includes fillings and root canal work as well as oral surgery and jaw setting. The fee due to the dentist for the supply of false teeth, including whole dentures, is authorized in each case by the regional sickness fund in accordance with a prescribed scale, on the basis of estimates prepared by the practitioner. Fund liability for payment, however, is limited according to the circumstances of each case and is capped as specified in fund bylaws. The insured has to pay any excess amount. The main association influences bylaws of the various regional sickness funds to such an extent that the standard of dental service is uniformly high throughout Austria.

Patients have complete freedom of choice over dentists. Dental treatment is provided by practitioners under contract to the patient's regional sickness fund or to a hospital similarly under contract. The dentist chosen by the insured person need not be under contract to the insured person's fund, but the patient in such cases must be prepared to settle fees and accept the amount eventually refunded by the fund.

Health insurance carriers are required to provide hospital accommodation, as well as all medical and nursing facilities needed by the insured, and to pay travel expenses for hospital attendance. Patients are entitled to receive in-patient treatment as long as they need it. Public hospitals have a legal obligation to admit insured persons whenever a doctor recommends admission. The insured is not obliged to contribute to the costs of a hospital stay, nor is the hospital entitled to exact payment. However, where a dependent of the insured receives hospital treatment (except because of a confinement), the insured is liable for 10 percent of daily hospital charges through the twenty-eighth day of hospitalization.

In-patient treatment is provided at the expense of the regional sickness fund as long as required and as long as the patient is covered by insurance (and fifty-two weeks thereafter if still a hospital in-patient on the date on which coverage expires). The fund's duty to provide hospital treatment also ceases if the insured, although still in need of personal attention, requires no further medical treatment—for example, if the disease for which he or she was being treated develops into a chronic incurable infirmity or into a mental ailment that is not susceptible to treatment.

Social insurance provides more than these various benefits in kind. As sickness is one of the main contingencies that interfere with earning a livelihood, Austria makes provision within the framework of compulsory health insurance for the payment of cash benefits in cases of incapacity for work as a result of illness. Incapacity is certified by the doctor who treated the insured. The sickness benefit is a cash benefit intended to help compensate for lost earnings. Insured persons are entitled to a sickness benefit for any day of incapacity for work that forms part of a period of interruption in employment. But no benefit is payable for the first three days of incapacity. The sickness benefit continues to be payable as long as the beneficiary satisfies the conditions of entitlement. It ceases to be payable after seventy-eight weeks. After right to the benefit is exhausted, it may not be paid again until the insured has requalified by no fewer than thirteen weeks in insurable employment.

Sickness benefits are paid at different rates, depending upon the treatment involved. If the insured is not receiving in-patient treatment, the sickness benefit is 50 percent of the contribution basis appropriate to the person's earnings; after incapacity for work has lasted forty-two days, the rate goes up to 60 percent, and if the insured has dependents it may go up to 75 percent.

If the insured is receiving in-patient treatment in a hospital, the sickness benefit is paid at a reduced rate, because the regional sickness fund is already paying board and lodging and thus relieving the insured of some normal costs of living.

Maternity benefits and death grants also involve cash payments. The Mothers' Protection Act requires expectant and nursing mothers to abstain from paid work from eight weeks before the expected date of confinement until the end of the eighth week following delivery. This postnatal period is extended to twelve weeks in cases of premature delivery, multiple births, and cesarean sections. A special maternity allowance is awarded to compensate women for earnings thus lost. The allowance is payable for time lost at work; the woman's own gynecologist is called upon to forecast the date of confinement. As maternity allowance is intended to replace earnings, it is paid only to women gainfully employed before they were required to cease work. It is the only social benefit whose size is determined by the amount of earnings (it is based on the average of earnings in the woman's last thirteen working weeks), even if such earnings exceed the ceilings applicable to contributions and benefits. The reason for such a drastic departure from normal practice is that maternity benefit is based on a special wish to promote family welfare. The regional sickness funds cover all costs arising in connection with a woman's confinement in a hospital, including all necessary travel expenses, a benefit in kind available to all insured persons and their dependents.

Finally, Austrian social insurance provides a death benefit in the form of a "death grant," payable by the regional sickness funds on the death of the insured person or any dependents, including a stillborn child. The death grant is payable at the rate of S6,000. Although ostensibly a contribution to funeral expenses, it is clearly insufficient to cover more than a fraction of actual burial costs.

Preventive Health Care

Insured persons are entitled to an annual medical checkup for themselves and their dependents. The regional sickness funds are also required to arrange the so-called "mother and child certificate" tests, as well as the medical examination of juveniles (persons between the ages of fifteen and eighteen). Juveniles are invited to have medical checkups at least once a year. The regional sickness funds have also recently been entrusted with human genetic screening, and it is intended that they should in the future perform certain types of vaccinations and inoculations.

Mention must also be made of miscellaneous measures designed to strengthen the health of the insured and dependents and to prevent future illness. These measures include the provision of recuperative facilities in convalescent homes and centers, spas, and other health resorts, as well as the payment of travel expenses. Sometimes the beneficiary is required to pay a share of the expenses involved. Occasionally the fund contributes to the cost of a stay at a health resort.

Industrial Injury Insurance

The primary objective of industrial injury insurance is to prevent accidents at work and industrial diseases and to counteract their effects on health. Victims of such accidents and diseases (hereafter the injured person) are to be rehabilitated in the sense of being as far as possible restored to their mental and physical condition prior to injury. This branch of statutory insurance also pays sums of money when injury results in the loss of income to the insured and dependents for a period of some length. A wide range of benefits, both in cash and in kind, are available. The law recognizes only two classes of contingencies that the scheme is required to meet, namely injury arising from an accident at work and injury resulting from an industrial disease. The scope of this branch of insurance has, however, been widened considerably with the passage of time, as we shall see.

The industrial injury insurance scheme in the ASVG applies to the employed, the farmers, and the self-employed alike. (Minor departures from arrangements laid down in the act are contained in a special piece of legislation relating to occupational injury insurance for civil servants.) In 1983 almost 4,800,000 persons were covered by statutory injury insurance. One and a quarter million were students, and 900,000 were self-employed. The number of accidents covered by this branch of insurance was about 270,000, of which 650 were fatal.

Originally industrial injury insurance could with some justification be regarded as a special and compulsory form of employers' liability insurance. The burden of paying contributions was exclusively the employers'. Although the scheme has been expanded to such a degree that it can no longer be regarded as applying exclusively to injuries sustained by employees in the course of their employment and at their place of work, sole responsibility for its operating funds is still borne by the employers. Employers are nowadays required to insure against accidents and diseases that they might themselves sustain or contract in the course of work, as well as to pay for the insurance of their staff.

With regard to benefits, it makes no difference whether injury is attributable to an accident at work or an industrial disease; benefits of the same description and the same size are provided in both instances. However, before we turn to those benefits, we need to look at the terms "accident at work" and "industrial disease." Accidents have an extraneous cause and are of limited duration; they result in a person's health being impaired. The injured person will get insurance benefits only if the accident arose from three types of activity: the pursuit of a gainful occupation, attendance at school or university, and the performance of acts in the interests of third parties.

Blue- and white-collar workers, miners, farmers, self-employed persons in commerce and industry, and so on, are all engaged in the pursuit of gainful occupations. They are thereby insured while performing tasks directly and causally connected with or related to their occupation. Insurance protection also covers accidents occurring on journeys to and from work, as well as on other work-related journeys. In agriculture and forestry insurance protection is particularly broad since there, more than anywhere else, occupational work and household work are almost indistinguishable. In recent years protection has been extended still further to include, for instance, accidents while employees are on their way to a midday meal outside the works premises or while attending meetings at the chamber of labor or trade union.

The extension of compulsory insurance to pupils and university students was preceded by a long debate between the political parties, because the extension threatened the idea that industrial injury insurance was introduced to relieve employers from liability to their employees. Today all pupils attending Austrian schools and all full-time university students of Austrian nationality are insured against accidents arising in the course of their studies, even if they take place outside educational premises (e.g., on a school outing) or occur during practical activities relating to the curriculum.

Acts performed in the interest of third parties, in order to qualify for insurance protection, must be done voluntarily and without thought of personal gain. They might aim to rescue, succor, and protect persons who are injured or in danger, or to avert or minimize serious damage to property. Members of various relief organizations, among them the voluntary fire service, the mountain rescue service, and the Red Cross, are thus insured against injury while working for these organizations.

Industrial diseases may be classified in two main categories. First, forty-four different diseases are listed in an annex to the ASVG. They are prescribed as industrial diseases in relation to certain occupations, which are likewise specified in the annex. Second, diseases caused by harmful substances and radiation but not mentioned in the annex may be accorded the status of industrial diseases if, on the basis of scientific research, the General Accident Insurance Carrier recommends and the federal minister for social affairs then endorses that finding. Thus the annex can be extended to new diseases as the need arises. In 1981 some 2,200 persons contracted industrial diseases, which in eleven cases proved fatal.

When an accident happens, the appropriate regional sickness fund is usually the first institution to provide treatment and to be involved from the insurance point of view. The fund thus provides a service that ought to be provided by one of the accident insurance carriers, and it does so because more often than not days if not weeks will elapse before a decision is made about whether the need for medical attention has arisen from an accident at work or from an event beyond the scope of industrial injury insurance. Accident treatment is similar in scope to the treatment provided under the (nonindustrial) health insurance scheme for ordinary disease.

For accident treatment the General Accident Insurance Carrier uses doctors with special skills and experience and provides treatment in one of its own hospitals. Seven special hospitals, and twenty-eight wards in general hospitals equipped to deal with injuries caused by industrial accidents, are available for in-patient, out-patient and day-patient treatment for nearly five million people who are insured against industrial accidents.

Cash benefits under the industrial injury insurance scheme are intended to compensate the injured and their dependents for loss of income. Many assessment bases are known in industrial injury insurance. For employed persons, the benefit basis is usually the injured person's reckonable earnings for the year immediately preceding the accident or the development of the disease. For self-employed persons in commerce and industry, farmers, pupils, and university students, the assessment basis is fixed by law. It is raised annually in line with percentage movements in average earnings.

The periodic payment of cash compensation to injured persons and dependents for loss of income is called "disablement pension." Its size (to be exact, the percentage rate by which the assessment basis applicable to the person concerned is multiplied) is graduated entirely according to how much the accident or disease has reduced the injured person's working capacity. Disablement pension is due as long as earning capacity has been reduced by at least 20 percent for a period exceeding three months (in the case of pupils and university students, earning capacity must have been reduced by at least 50 percent). Pensions may be redetermined in order to take account of changes in medical condition. If there are no such changes, pensions will be paid until the death of the disabled; it is also possible to convert a pension into a lump-sum payment.

In the case of a total loss of earning capacity, disablement pension is payable at the rate of two-thirds of the assessment basis. Such a pension is called "full pension." (The monthly amount of pension is equal to one-fourteenth of the annual pension and is payable fourteen times a year.) Other pensions are prorated according to the degree of earning capacity the pensioner has lost. But any injured person whose earning capacity is reduced by at least 50 percent will have his or her pension increased by 20 percent, so that a full pension in fact amounts to 80 percent of the assessment basis.

The pension of the injured person is increased by 10 percent for each dependent child. The recipient of a full pension so severely disabled as to need constant attention will be awarded an additional "constant attendance allowance."

Survivors' benefits in the form of pensions are only payable when death is attributable to an accident at work or an industrial disease. The following dependents may be eligible for survivors' pensions: widows and widowers, orphaned children, and parents and grandparents as well as brothers and sisters. The total of all survivors' pensions may in the aggregate not exceed 80 percent of the deceased's assessment basis. Parents, grandparents, brothers, and sisters are entitled to survivors' pensions only if the deceased contributed wholly or mainly to the cost of their maintenance; moreover, to be eligible, parents and grandparents must be destitute and brothers and sisters unprovided for. The total of pensions paid to this group of dependents may in the aggregate not exceed 20 percent of the assessment basis applicable to the deceased.

In addition to these various classes of pensions, which are in principle payable for an indefinite time, there are also cash benefits payable only for a limited period. An injured person receiving accident treatment and in consequence unable to go to work is entitled to injury benefit—the equivalent of sickness benefit, although the rates at which it is payable are higher. (Both sickness and injury benefits are payable at different rates, according to whether the injured person is receiving out-patient or in-patient treatment.) Special assistance in the form of cash payments may be made available to injured persons if their disablement is severe and can be expected to persist for a long time. While undergoing rehabilitation the injured person is entitled to a provisional allowance, which is intended to compensate for lost earnings during rehabilitation; additional financial help may also be granted to help speed the return to work.

The law requires accident insurance carriers to set up special accident prevention departments and to provide suitably qualified officers to run them. These officers are authorized to inspect industrial, commercial, and agricultural premises to determine whether existing arrangements ensure a reasonable safety standard for the work force. They are obliged to warn owners of their proposed visits and to work in close cooperation with officials of the local factory inspectorate.

If in specific cases persons are in danger of contracting an industrial disease, and the danger is confirmed by medical opinion, the appropriate accident insurance carrier may provide preventive treatment in the form of recuperative facilities. Such preventive measures are made available on an ex gratia basis; they cannot be claimed as of right. The range of preventive measures is wide enough to include the payment of pensions for up to two years so that a worker at risk can change careers and be compensated for lost earnings in the meantime.

The payment of benefit under the industrial injury scheme can be suspended only in exceptional circumstances (during a term of imprisonment or a stay outside Austria). It is important to note that the receipt of a disablement pension does not disqualify the recipient from simultaneously receiving an old age pension or an invalidism pension under the pension insurance scheme. Both classes of pension are due to those who qualify for both without abatement.

Pension Insurance

Pension insurance is designed to meet the contingencies of old age, reduced working capacity, and death, mainly by making provision for the periodic payment of long-term cash benefits (pensions). Benefits in kind, of secondary importance, are provided in the form of preventive health care to forestall the need to pay invalidism pensions.

The pension arrangements applicable to white-collar workers differ slightly from those for blue-collar workers, and in particular from those for workers in the mining industry.

Two kinds of conditions must be fulfilled for benefits to be awarded.

The first include conditions that have to be met in each and every case, regardless of the particular benefit claimed (universal conditions). One of these universal conditions is the requirement that the claimant's insurance record be of a minimum length (waiting period). The term insurance record, or insurance period, can mean either a contribution period or an equivalent period, the former a period for which payment has been made, the latter a period for which payment was not made but which is treated as equivalent to a contribution period. In some cases the insurance periods must be distributed in a certain manner during the time the claimant was gainfully employed. The other universal condition requires the claimant to have retired from work on a certain day, called the *key day* (*Stichtag*). The second includes "special conditions" that are not of universal application and that vary according to the class of benefit being claimed. Examples of special conditions include attainment of the pensionable age in the case of an old age pension; unemployment or a lengthy insurance record (thirty-five years or more) in the case of "premature" old age pension; reduction in working capacity in the case of invalidism pension; and death in the case of survivors' benefits.

The key day mentioned above is the first day of the calendar month following the filing of a pension claim. It is the date on which all conditions, whether universal or special, prescribed in respect of the benefit claimed must have been met if the benefit in question is to be awarded. To satisfy the prescribed contribution conditions, a claimant must in the first place have completed (in insurance parlance, "acquired") the waiting period before being entitled to the benefit claimed. In the case of old age pensions of any description the waiting period—that is, the minimum number of reckonable insurance months—is 180 months. The waiting period for all other pensions is 60 months if the claimant is not fifty-five (male) or fifty (female) years old on the key day. If he or she is older, the waiting period reflects his or her greater age; for example, for a man 58 years old on the key day, the waiting period is 60 plus 36 months for a total of 96 months.

The conditions governing the award of a premature old age pension on the grounds of lengthy insurance are more stringent: the claimant must have acquired at least twenty-four contribution months of compulsory insurance in the thirty-six months preceding the key day.

A pension is regarded as the replacement of lost earnings. From such a view follows the requirement that on the key day the claimant must not be in any gainful occupation involving insurance liability; in other words, the claimant must have retired from normal work by that date (trivial earnings are disregarded). If the pensioner subsequently takes on insurable work, payment of part of the pension will be withheld until the pensioner retires from the new occupation.

A few words still need to said about the equivalent periods. The most important of these equivalent periods are the following: periods of war service or captivity, of service with the Austrian armed forces, of unemployment, of sickness, and of schooling and vocational training, as well as (for mothers) the first twelve months following the delivery of a child. Armed with this knowledge of the basic concepts of Austrian social insurance law, we can now discuss the several benefits that the law makes available.

Pension Insurance Benefits

Old age benefit is normally due at age sixty-five in the case of men, age sixty in the case of women. The two forms of premature old age pension (on grounds of unemployability or long insurance record—the latter case is known as "early pension") pensionable age is sixty for men and fifty-five for women.

To be eligible for premature pension on the grounds of unemployment, the claimant (who must of course fulfill all other conditions prescribed for the award of an old age pension) must have received unemployment or sickness benefit for at least one year during the fifteen months immediately preceding the key day. This kind of pension implicitly recognizes that elderly people once unemployed or sick for a whole year have virtually no hope of again finding suitable employment. Early pension on grounds of a long insurance record is payable to claimants who have acquired at least 450 insurance months. Such an insurance record reflects lifelong work in insurable employment. Because of these variations, in a good many cases it is up to the insured to make up his or her mind whether to retire early or to carry on until reaching normal pension age.

A pioneering law came into effect on July 1, 1981, lowering pensionable age to fifty-seven in the case of insured persons performing arduous work involving night shifts (e.g., underground work in collieries or in plants where excessive heat and noise are generated) after they have been so engaged for specified periods of time. The pension (known as "early retirement pay") due to such workers is equal to the invalidism pension to which they would have been entitled if, on the date of their retirement, they had been invalids within the meaning of the law. From the worker's sixtieth birthday onward, this early retirement pay is converted into a regular old age pension. This special scheme is financed by contributions payable by the owners of the industrial establishments concerned and from the public purse. Other measures were introduced simultaneously: an increased number of breaks during working hours, special holidays, and other recuperative facilities. These will, it is hoped, minimize the adverse effects of arduous night work on the health of workers to an extent that will allow the gradual withdrawal of the early retirement pay scheme by the end of 1990. The Special Benefit Act, mentioned earlier, also allows retirement before normal pension age if warranted by special circumstances laid down in the act. And indeed, over the last few years the tendency to retire on pension before reaching normal pensionable age has become increasingly common.

Table 5.6 sets out the various classes of old age pensions paid in 1984. The size of pension depends on two factors: the assessment basis, which is the size of the insured person's insurable earnings during the ten years preceding the date of retirement (a consequence of the pension reform beginning in 1987), and the length of insurance record. The aim of this calculation is to provide a pension so closely related to most recent earnings that retirement from work does not involve too sharp a drop in standard of living. Although the gross pension is not very much lower than final gross earnings, the gap between the two net amounts is even narrower. A pensioner is not required to pay more than 3 percent of the pension for health insurance, nor does he or she have to pay social insurance contributions of any kind; the pension, in the nature of things smaller than earnings, is therefore taxed at a lower rate than earnings. Needless to say, these observations are valid only when the insured person's earnings do not greatly exceed the ceiling on earnings applicable to contributions and consequently to the size of the benefit. It must not be forgotten, however, that the size of pensions may be increased by the voluntary payment of contributions for supplementary insurance.

The earnings of many workers, particularly manual laborers, reach their peak at the height of their physical fitness and not at the end of their working lives. The law recognizes this fact by allowing the insured person's earnings during the five years immediately preceding his or her forty-fifth birthday to determine the assessment basis for the calculation of a great portion of the pension. Pensions are generally calculated by the method that produces the higher pension for the insured. Without going into the details, we should mention that miners get higher benefits in their old age pensions than do blue- and white-collar workers in general.

A pension is made up of the assessment basis and an increment rate. This rate is determined by the number of insurance months that the insured has acquired: 1.9 percent of the assessment basis is due for every year up to thirty and 1.5 percent for each subsequent year. As no more than 540 months (forty-five years) may be taken into account for calculating the amount of pension, the maximum rate of pension equals 79.5 percent of the assessment basis. The pension so calculated is payable fourteen times a year.

This system has been in effect since January 1, 1985. Previously, a pension was made up of two elements: a flat rate of 30.0 percent of the assessment basis and an incremental rate of 6.0 percent of the basis for the first ten years of insurance, 9.0 percent for the second decade, 12.0 percent for the third, 15.0 percent for the fourth, and 1.5 percent for each subsequent year (totaling 79.5 percent of the assessment basis). Under the new system, pension determination depends more on elements of pure insurance: a short insurance period now gives a small pension, because there is no longer a flat rate, and a long insurance period gives a high pension.

Invalidism benefits are payable in the form of pensions if the working capacity of the insured has been reduced to below a certain prescribed level. Among blue-collar workers other than miners a slight distinction in the matter of invalidism is made between skilled and unskilled workers. A skilled worker is deemed an invalid if accident or disease reduces his or her capacity for work to less than half the working capacity of a person of similar skills whose physical and mental condition is normal (i.e., who can work at the job for which he or she has received professional training). The criteria for white-collar workers are identical to those for skilled blue-collar workers. An unskilled worker (one who has no qualifications and abilities characteristic of a specific occupation) is deemed an invalid if he or she is no longer able to earn at least half the amount that healthy persons can, working without restriction on kind of job or industry.

Persons employed in the mining industry are in a similar legal posi-

TABLE 5.6

Average Number of Old Age Pensions Paid in 1984, by Carrier (in schillings)

Type of Pension	Employed	Self-Employed in Commerce and Industry	Farmers, Foresters	Total
Normal	477,600(82.8%)	64,900(89.8%)	63,500(88.0%)	606,000(84.0%)
Premature	12,500(2.2)	—	—	12,500(1.7)
Early	86,700(15.0)	7,400(10.2)	8,700(12.0)	102,800(14.3)
Total	576,800(100.0)	72,300(100.0)	72,200(100.0)	721,300(100.0)

Note: Normal pensions are those paid at the customary retirement age; premature pensions are payable to those deemed unemployable by reason of age or persistent ill health; and early pensions are payable to those who choose to retire early and with a long record of regular, insurable work.

TABLE 5.7

Equalization Supplement Recipients in 1983, by Carrier

Type of Pension Supplemented	Employed	Self-Employed in Commerce and Industry	Farmers, Foresters	All
Invalidism	58,590(23.6%)	4,727(28.5%)	13,768(28.7%)	77,085(24.7%)
Old age	45,690(8.2)	13,508(18.8)	25,984(35.3)	85,182(12.1)
Widow, widower	78,488(21.2)	16,119(37.2)	25,070(56.0)	119,677(26.1)
Orphan	12,049(20.7)	1,286(23.4)	3,786(41.8)	17,121(23.5)

Note: The number of recipients as a percentage of pensioners is shown in parentheses.

tion. A miner, however, though still fit for work and even earning more than half what co-workers earn, will nevertheless be entitled to a (reduced) invalidism pension if prevented by illness from doing the kind of work performed previously. In such cases the invalidism pension is designed to compensate the recipient for the fact that he or she can no longer work at a former, more remunerative job. A miner who becomes an invalid in the wider meaning explained earlier is entitled to an ordinary invalidism pension.

The waiting period for the award of an invalidism pension—as noted—is five years (60 months); it is extended up to fifteen years (180 months) in cases where an insured person was over the age of fifty (women) or fifty-five (men) on the key day. Invalidism pensions are calculated in the same way as old age pensions, but with one exception. Where such a calculation would result in a pension of less than 50 percent of the assessment basis, the incremental rate is increased for claimants who have not turned fifty years of age on the key day. For every twelve months between the key day and the first day following the claimant's fiftieth birthday, the incremental rate is raised by 1.9 percent to a maximum of 50.0 percent. For example, a thirty-year-old male worker with ten insurance years would qualify for 19 percent of the assessment basis; for the twenty years between his thirtieth and fiftieth years he receives a bonus of 38 percent, reduced in the event to 31 percent because 50 percent is the maximum permissible.

Death benefits include survivors' pensions for widows, widowers, and orphaned children, as well as lump-sum payments. A widow's pension is payable to the lawfully wedded wife of an insured person at the time of his death. A widow's pension, however, is also due to the wife of an earlier marriage, to the extent that the insured was legally bound to maintain her. The conditions for the award of widow's pension are more stringent when the insured was over the age of sixty-five when the marriage was contracted. In order to discourage "pension marriages," the law demands that a marriage must have existed for a minimum length of time—the actual length is proportionate to the difference in age between the spouses—before a widow's pension may be awarded to the survivor.

A widow's pension equals 60 percent of the pension due to the deceased or, if he died while still gainfully employed, that would have been due to him if at the time of his death he had qualified for an invalidism pension. The minimum rate of widow's pension, however, is not less than 30 percent of the assessment basis applicable to the deceased. The wife of an earlier marriage is entitled to a widow's pension that does not exceed the monthly payment specified for maintenance by court order, or by agreement in court, or under terms of a contract executed before the marriage was terminated. The pension due to the wife of an earlier marriage may not exceed the pension to which a widow is entitled. A woman loses her right to widow's pension on remarriage, but in such a case she is entitled to a gratuity equal to thirty-five months of pension.

Legislation effective June 1, 1981 put men and women on a footing of absolute equality in the area of survivors' benefits. Thus the husband of an earlier marriage is also entitled to a widower's benefit when he fulfills the conditions that the wife of an earlier marriage must satisfy to claim a widow's pension. Equality is being phased in, however, and only in 1995 will the widower's pension be paid at the full rate; benefit inequalities between the two sexes will persist until then.

Children of the deceased are entitled to orphaned children's pensions. Such pensions are payable at 40 percent of the widow's or widower's pension if the child loses one parent, 60 percent if both parents die.

Provision is made within the framework of the pension insurance scheme for various supplementary payments and allowances to account for the fact that the manner in which the pension is calculated may, for the claimant with a short insurance record and low earnings immediately before retirement, result in a benefit below subsistence levels. To spare needy pensioners the embarrassment of having to apply for public assistance, the ASVG introduces a special supplement, called the *equalization supplement*, which is intended to bring pensions up to subsistence level. (In 1985 monthly amounts of S4,514 in the case of single persons and S6,466 in the case of a married couple, plus S481 for each child, were regarded as sufficient to meet basic needs.) In cases where the pension plus the aggregate of the pensioner's other income and the income of his or her spouse fall short of the subsistence amounts, the pensioner is entitled to an equalization supplement large enough to bridge the difference. The costs involved in such payments are met by the federal government, which reimburses the pension insurance carriers for their expenses in the matter of the supplement. Table 5.7 shows the extent to which equalization supplements were paid by the end of 1983.

Pensions are increased for each child of the beneficiary. This child benefit equals 5 percent of the beneficiary's assessment basis, subject to minimum and maximum amounts. In 1985 these amounts were S217 and S650 per month. The child benefit is payable in addition to the family allowances due under the Family Burden Equalization Scheme.

A pensioner who is in such a poor state of health as to be entirely or almost entirely dependent upon outside help is entitled to a constant attendance allowance. This allowance takes the form of an increase in pension intended to help meet some of the extra expenses incurred as the result of helplessness. The maximum and minimum rates at which this allowance was paid in 1985 were S2,627 and S2,266 per month.

In common with the industrial injury insurance scheme, and with the same ends, the pension insurance system provides rehabilitation facilities in order to prevent insured persons from becoming invalids and thereby pensioners before their time. Rehabilitation facilities may to a limited extent also be made available to the dependents of the insured, but only if the institutions and centers concerned, which are administered by the various pension insurance carriers, are able to admit them and if the insured would otherwise be exposed to excessive financial liabilities.

All insured persons and pensioners, including recipients of old age pensions, may, under the pension insurance scheme, be granted preventive health care (stays in health resorts and accomodation in recuperative and rehabilitation centers). Through such roundabout methods, rehabilitation, admittedly of a somewhat limited sort, may be provided even to beneficiaries who receive old age pensions. Travel expenses and transportation costs are included in rehabilitation benefits. So are preventative health care and the supply of orthopedic appliances, as well as necessary alterations and adaptations in the home (e.g., the installation of handrails). All these facilities are granted on an ex gratia basis.

Adjustment of Cash Benefits

The flexible nature of the Austrian social insurance system, with its annual review of contributions and their automatic adjustment to current wage trends, has already been noted. The analogous adjustment of benefits to current economic conditions raises complicated financial issues, because such adjustments are bound to increase the size of benefits and thereby of expenditures. To avoid a cost explosion and to keep expenditures within reasonable limits, the law here departs from the principle of automatic adjustment. Benefits are not linked by law to the revaluation coefficient by which contributions are increased, and benefits need not necessarily be increased at the same rate as contributions are. Instead, a special benefits coefficient has been introduced. It is worked out year by year by a special advisory council, consisting of representatives of both sides of industry and independent experts. In its report to the federal minister for social affairs the council specifies in a percentage the coefficient that in its opinion should be applied to existing benefits in the ensuing year. The council's recommedations are not binding, but a minister fixing the coefficient at a different rate must state the reasons for the change. The ministerial regulation that determines the coefficient must be approved by the government as a whole and must then be endorsed by the main committee of Parliament, a procedure clearly designed to secure the widest possible political backing. Although, for these reasons, the benefits coefficient need not necessarily be identical with the contribution coefficient, the two coefficients have in practice been identical for the last twenty years, and there has been no disagreement between the advisory council and the federal minister for social affairs.

The revaluation of benefits has given pensioners over the last twenty years a chance to participate in the economic advances of the working population, which is in all probability why the current pension system meets with general approval. Table 5.8 shows how benefits have kept pace with the Austrian consumer price index.

Payment of Benefits

Benefits are payable monthly (twice in May and October) and in advance. Several legal provisions forbid or restrict the execution of liens against social insurance benefits. Benefits are paid through the mail at the expense of the insurance carrier.

PROCEDURES, APPEALS, AND ENFORCEMENT OF CLAIMS

In their relations with the insured, their dependents, and employers liable for contributions, social insurance carriers occupy a position akin to that of a public authority of the state. They are entitled to exact contri-

TABLE 5.8
Annual Increases in Pensions and Consumer Prices, 1965–83

Year	Monthly Pension (S[a])	Increase in Pensions	Increase in Cost of Living	Increase in Purchasing Power
1965	2,000.00	—	—	—
1966	2,140.00	7.0%	2.2%	4.7%
1967	2,313.30	8.1	4.0	3.9
1968	2,461.40	6.4	2.8	3.5
1969	2,636.20	7.1	3.1	3.9
1970	2,778.60	5.4	4.4	1.0
1971	2,975.90	7.1	4.7	2.3
1972	3,196.10	7.4	6.3	1.0
1973	3,483.70	9.0	7.6	1.3
1974[b]	3,846.00			
1974[c]	3,961.40	12.1	9.5	2.5
1975[d]	4,365.50			
1975[c]	4,496.50	13.5	8.4	4.7
1976[e]	5,013.60	13.1	7.3	5.4
1977	5,364.60	7.0	5.5	1.4
1978	5,734.80	6.9	3.6	3.2
1979	6,107.60	6.5	3.7	2.7
1980	6,449.60	5.6	6.4	− 0.8
1981	6,778.50	5.1	6.8	− 1.6
1982	7,131.00	5.2	5.4	− 0.2
1983	7,523.20	5.5	3.3	2.1
Multiyear Interval Increases (cumulative)				
1965–70		38.9	17.6	18.1
1970–75		59.4	42.1	12.2
1975–80		45.6	29.4	12.5
1970–80		132.1	83.9	26.2
1970–83		170.8	113.9	26.6

Notes: a. Amount where pension started in 1962 or earlier.
     b. Increase by 10.4%.
     c. Increase by 3.0%.
     d. Increase by 10.2%.
     e. Increase on January 1, 1976, by 11.5%.

butions from the insured and where applicable from their employers; they allow or disallow benefits; they are authorized to insist on the refund of excess payments they have made in error; and they can take legal action against the individual in several other matters. The individual must therefore be in a position to challenge apparent injustices at the hands of a social insurance carrier. Admittedly, social insurance carriers are organized as self-governing bodies; protection of the individual, after all, furnishes the main reason for administering social insurance by representatives of the insured. But even representatives make mistakes. Moreover, given the sheer volume of business and numbers of staff, these "representatives" cannot superintend the work of the carrier in every detail. Despite self-administration, therefore, it has proved necessary to introduce special procedural rules that enable the insured to contest decisions made by the carriers.

The procedural steps binding on the administrative authorities are rather cumbersome and would if indiscriminately applied paralyze the carriers' operations. Hence a simpler and quicker form of procedure is allowed. (If a person is dissatisfied with the outcome of such simplified procedures of factfinding, he or she is at liberty to object to it.) Moreover, the general rule requiring administrative authorities to clothe their decisions in the style of formal decrees has been relaxed; in many cases the carrier can proceed on an entirely informal basis. For example, medical service and the reimbursement of the costs of treatment are provided without the issue of formal decrees.

If the decree (or its informal equivalent decision) issued by a public authority is not contested by way of appeal within a period of time set by law, it enters into final and irrevocable effect. At that point, the subject of the decree is conclusively settled, and the decree is binding upon all the concerned parties. Only in the most blatant cases is the principle of absolute finality allowed to be overruled. For example, proceedings may be resumed in cases where fresh and importance evidence comes to light or where one of the parties concerned in the proceedings is shown to have obtained a decree by fraudulent means.

Departures from the absolute finality of decrees in favor of the insured are numerous and of far-reaching effect. Thus a social insurance carrier, discovering a substantial error of fact or of interpretation in the proceeding leading to a decree, is obliged to take the initiative itself to put matters right and even, where appropriate, pay retroactive cash benefits to the claimant. In contrast, the law states that payments a carrier makes by mistake can be reclaimed only if the recipient is largely to blame for the overpayment or could reasonably have been expected to recognize that an overpayment had been made. Even when a carrier is entitled to insist on a refund, it must do so within two years of the original error.

Procedural problems are likely to arise in the case of benefits tied to a statutorily defined degree of lost earning capacity. The carriers concerned with the administration of industrial injury insurance award pensions on the basis of diminished earning capacity first on a provisional basis, for a maximum of two years, without being permanently committed to the terms of the provisional decision. Thus, the carriers can provide quick aid with a minimum of bureaucratic effort while avoiding the risk that mistakes (easy to make because of the speed of the procedure) might become irremediable. But once the final industrial injury pension has been determined by decree, and the decree has entered into final effect, the pension may be varied only on the grounds that the recipient's earning capacity has substantially improved or worsened. If the carrier mistakenly and through no fault of the insured fixes by decree the pension at a rate higher than warranted by circumstances, that pension may be neither withdrawn nor reduced once the decree in question has come into final effect.

An individual dissatisfied with the manner in which a carrier deals with a claim or other legal right may contest the decision either by appeal or by instituting legal proceedings. Social insurance law makes a sharp distinction between decisions relating to benefits (i.e., decisions by which a claim to benefit or the duty to refund payments are admitted or denied) and decisions relating to administrative issues. The latter decisions mainly concern disputes about alleged eligibility to enroll in social insurance and, if a person is eligible, how much he or she should be required to pay in contributions and to which of the carriers.

Decisions relating to administrative issues can be overturned by procedures that social insurance law models on ordinary administrative procedures. Appeal goes to the next highest authority (provincial governor, federal minister for social affairs). The jurisdiction of the Adminstrative High Court may also be invoked after all the remedies provided by administrative law have been exhausted.

In the case of decrees relating to benefits special courts, wrongly known as social insurance arbitration tribunals, have been established to enable individuals, by bringing an action against a carrier, to have offending decrees rescinded and claims redetermined by the court. The action that an aggrieved claimant brings against the carrier that issued the offending decree automatically rescinds the decree, so that in the eyes of the Constitutional High Court there is no infringement of the constitutional principle that the judicial function should be strictly differentiated from that of the executive. Since the decree of the social insurance carrier is automatically set aside, proceedings before the tribunal represent a fresh start.

The automatic rescision of contested decrees does not, however, serve to revive earlier decrees. Such a principle, if allowed to take effect without qualification, might give rise to great hardship in individual cases. Consider, for example, an insured man who was awarded a pension for 60 percent loss of earning capacity. Subsequently, on the assumption that his state of health has improved, the pension is reduced to 30 percent. Dissatisfied with this state of affairs, he brings an action in the local social insurance tribunal against the carrier that issued the decree which reduced his pension. His bringing action automatically sets aside the latter decree—but the former decree, which had awarded him the original 60 percent pension, is not revived. Pending the court's finding as to the size of the pension due to him, he is entitled to no pension at all. To avoid such situations, the law obliges the carrier, pending the outcome of proceedings, to continue to pay the pension at the rate laid down in the contested decree. These and other complications result from the attempt to respect the principle of the independence and separation of the executive and the judiciary as laid down in the Austrian Constitution.

Proceedings in the arbitration tribunals are inexpensive as far as claimants are concerned. Claimants need not engage lawyers to represent them; they may plead their cases themselves or allow themselves to be represented by officials, skilled in the kind of litigation involved, of the organizations that represent their economic or professional interests. Trial costs, including fees payable to medical expert witnesses, are borne by the carrier that is being sued.

Usually, it does not take the tribunals long to arrive at a finding. In most trials the issue at stake is the size of payments allegedly due to the insured on account of some bodily or mental injury involving lost earning capacity. Thus it is seldom a point of law but usually the assessment of the plaintiff's state of health that needs to be established, and the medical expert plays first fiddle in the proceedings.

Social insurance arbitration tribunals have been set up in each of the nine provinces. The tribunal sits in benches of two lay assessors and one professional judge who presides over the trial. The professional judges are not specialists in social insurance law; in point of fact, their work on these tribunals is usually a sideline for them, performed on a part-time basis and in addition to their main function in other courts of law. The social partnership organizations each nominate a certain number of potential lay assessors. The names are entered on two lists, and it is from these panels that the presiding judge selects the assessors needed for the trial before the proceeding commences. Lay assessors have the same right to vote as the presiding judge; their participation in the trial is intended to strengthen the plaintiff's confidence in the impartiality of the tribunal and to give the professional judge the benefit of practical skills and vocational experience.

The judgments of the tribunals may be contested by way of appeal to the Court of Appeal in Vienna, whose decisions in social insurance matters are final and not subject to further appeal. When hearing appeals in social insurance matters, the Court of Appeal in Vienna sits in benches composed exclusively of professional judges who are specialists in social insurance law. At trial before the court, the insured must be represented by a member of the legal profession.

New legislation will modify the procedural elements of social insurance law beginning in 1987, but there will be no substantial change in practice.

International Social Insurance Law

Bilateral Relations

The scope of a social security convention is limited by the branch of insurance that it seeks to cover and the class of persons to which it applies. Table 5.9 lists the conventions in force between Austria and various other countries (supplementary conventions are not listed) as of 1985. The table also specifies the type or types of insurance included in each convention. On the whole, the nationals of the contracting countries as well as their dependents and survivors are always included in the personal realm of the convention. Some conventions, though not all, extend the arrangements provided to resident political refugees and stateless persons.

TABLE 5.9

Bilateral Social Insurance Conventions,
by Austrian Social Insurance Legislation

Other Country (date of effect)	Employed	Self-employed in Commerce and Industry	Farmers	Civil Servants[a]	Unemployment	Family Allowances
Yugoslavia (Jan 67)	yes	—	—	[b]	yes	yes
Switzerland (Jan 69)	yes[c]	[e]	[e]	[f]	yes[g]	yes
Liechtenstein (Mar 69)	[d]	[d]	[d]	—	yes[h]	yes
Turkey (Oct 69)	yes	yes	yes	yes	—	yes
West Germany (Nov 69)	yes	yes	yes	yes	yes[i]	yes
France (Nov 72)	yes	yes	yes	yes	—	yes
Luxemburg (Jan 74)	yes	yes	yes	yes	yes	yes
Netherlands (Jan 75)	yes	yes	yes	yes	yes	yes
Israel (Jan 75)	yes[j]	yes[j]	yes[j]	yes[j]	yes	yes
Sweden (Nov 76)	yes	yes	yes	yes	yes	yes

TABLE 5.9 (*Continued*)

Other Country (date of effect)	Employed	Self-employed in Commerce and Industry	Farmers	Civil Servants[a]	Unemployment	Family Allowances
Belgium (Dec 78)	yes	yes	yes	yes	yes	yes
Great Britain (May 81)	yes	yes	yes	yes	yes	yes
Greece (Oct 81)	yes	yes	yes	yes	yes	yes
Philippines (Apr 82)	k	k	k	l	—	—
Italy (Jul 83)	yes	yes	yes	yes	yes	yes
Spain (Jul 83)	yes	yes	yes	yes	yes	yes

Notes: a. Health and Occupational Injury Act for Civil Servants.
b. Only health insurance.
c. In the area of health insurance, only the change from the system of one country to that of the other is facilitated.
d. Only pension insurance.
e. Industrial injury and pension insurance.
f. Only industrial injury insurance.
g. Separate convention of December 14, 1978.
h. Separate convention of July 24, 1981.
i. Separate convention of July 19, 1978.
j. In the area of health insurance, only maternity benefits.
k. Industrial injury insurance (limited to the remittance of pensions and other cash benefits) and pension insurance.
l. Only industrial injury insurance, limited to the remittance of pensions and other cash benefits.

The principle of nondiscrimination in social insurance is at the core of every such convention. It provides that nationals of one contracting party, when in the territory of the other party, should be treated concerning their rights and obligations in the same way as nationals of the other party. A convention that covers political refugees and stateless persons will, as a rule, apply the principle of nondiscrimination to these classes of persons only if they are ordinarily resident in the territory of one of the two parties. Since Austrian social insurance law does not discriminate between Austrians and non-Austrians, and thus is applicable to anyone resident (permanently or otherwise) in Austria, the nondiscrimination clauses in social security conventions have no special significance in Austrian domestic law.

Bilateral social security conventions regard the territories of the two contracting parties as forming one single territory insofar as legislation to which the convention specifically applies is concerned and insofar as this one-unit principle is compatible with the terms of the convention. This principle is particularly significant for the export of benefits and in relation to claims by non-Austrians for benefits from the Austrian social insurance system. In industrial injury and pension insurance, the principle implies that a pension payable under the law of one contracting party cannot be suspended when the recipient is in the territory of the other party. In health insurance (when included in a convention) it implies that a national of a contracting party who needs medical attention and treatment when inside Austria will frequently be entitled to receive them under the same conditions as an Austrian national with health insurance. The extent of entitlement, however, varies between those whose stay in Austria is only temporary and permanent residents of Austria. The former are entitled to claim medical attention and treatment only in case of emergency, while the latter are under no such restriction. Permanent residents can make unrestricted use of the Austrian health insurance system only if they can show that they have obtained the consent of the insurance authorities in their country of nationality to their taking up residence in Austria. Persons entitled to a pension under the legislation of the other contracting party are, if permanent residents of Austria, frequently entitled to receive medical attention and treatment under the same conditions as Austrian pensioners. Insurance authorities in the territory of the party that provides medical care in these circumstances will, as a rule, be entitled to obtain a refund of its costs (but not its administrative expenses) from the insurance authority in the territory of the other party.

Pension insurance invariably presents the central problem of every social security convention. These conventions commonly aggregate insurance periods completed under the legislation of both parties. Thus for the purpose of determining whether a person is entitled to a pension under the legislation of one or the other party, or under the legislation of both, the insurance record of the person concerned may be composed of periods acquired under the legislation of one or the other party or both (it goes without saying that whether a certain period will qualify for inclusion in that record is decided by the authorities in the territory of the party under whose law it is supposed to have been completed).

When a person is entitled to receive a pension under the legislation of one party, the competent insurance authority of that party first determines the notional full pension due to the claimant had the claimant completed the entire insurance record under its legislation. That part of the notional full pension actually completed within the former party is the actual as distinct from the notional pension that the insurance authority will pay. A similar calculation is carried out by the competent insurance authority within the other territory. The following example illustrates this seemingly complicated procedure. Assume a man had been in insurable employment for thirty years in Austria and for ten years in a foreign country with which Austria maintains bilateral relations in social security. The Austrian insurance carrier, when confronted with a pension claim by the person concerned, would first calculate the amount of pension due to him if all forty years had been worked under Austrian law. Let us assume that this calculation produces a notional pension of S8,000 a month. But because only three-quarters of the claimant's years of insurance were completed under the Austrian system, the Austrian insurance carrier is required to pay only three-quarters of the notional pension, that is, S6,000 per month. The insurance authority in the territory of the other party proceeds in the same manner and eventually pays the claimant one-quarter of the notional pension he would have received had he worked all forty years within the territory of the other party. Thus, briefly, in each country the amount of pension due to the claimant is fixed *pro rata temporis*.

Insofar as social security conventions relate to industrial injury and disease, they primarily claim that if a person sustained an industrial injury or contracted an industrial disease to which the legislation of one of the contracting parties applies and later on sustains an industrial injury or contracts an industrial disease to which the legislation of the other contracting party applies, then for the purpose of determining the loss of earning capacity and thereby the right to pension under the rules of the latter party, account should be taken of the former injury or disease as though the legislation of the latter party had applied to it. The actual size of the pension payable in these circumstances, however, is determined solely by the degree of lost earning capacity due to the later injury or disease. Benefits in kind are, on the whole, provided in the same way that similar benefits are provided under health insurance. A national of one party who sustains an industrial injury or contracts an industrial disease in the territory of the other party will in all probability return to the territory of the former party for medical care. The insurance authority concerned will obtain a refund for its costs in such cases from its counterpart.

The effectiveness of the bilateral social security arrangements in force between Austria and other countries can be judged from the statistics. In 1983 benefits of unlimited duration in the amount of S30 billion were remitted to Austria by the insurance authorities of foreign countries; Austria exported some S20 billion in the same year.

Austria has also concluded bilateral conventions with the United Nations Industrial Development Organization, the European Organization for Nuclear Research, the International Atomic Energy Agency, and the United Nations High Commissioner for Refugees concerning social security for officials based in Austria. All four conventions exempt staff from paying Austrian social insurance contributions provided that they are covered by the United Nations Joint Staff Pensions Fund. At the same time, the conventions allow staff to pay voluntary contributions under the Austrian health and unemployment insurance schemes. Those members of staff not covered by the United Nations Joint Staff Pensions Fund are subject to compulsory insurance (including unemployment insurance) under Austrian law unless they are covered by the social security system of another country.

Finally, an administrative regulation of the Federal Ministry for Social Affairs lays down that where a national of Austria or of the United States would be entitled to a benefit (other than a premature old age pension) payable under Austrian pension insurance law if inside Austria, he or she should be entitled to receive that benefit while in the

United States. Furthermore, a United States national entitled to any benefit payable under Austrian law if inside Austria is entitled to receive that benefit (with the consent of the competent Austrian insurance authority) while within the territory of a country other than the United States. Austrian authorities do not, as a rule, withhold their consent.

Multilateral Relations

The large number of sovereign states in Europe is largely responsible for the relatively limited capacity of each of the several national labor markets. This aspect, coupled with striking differences in the structures of the national economies in Northern and Southern Europe (economists speak of a "North-South gradient"), helps account for the movement of labor from one country to another within Europe. In the early 1980s an estimated 10 million migrant workers, some 8 to 9 percent of the total European labor force, were employed away from their own countries in one of the traditionally receiving countries of Europe.

Multilateral conventions, like bilateral arrangements, seek to safeguard the social insurance interests of workers in insurable employment in two or more countries. Their primary aim is to ensure that migrant workers enjoy the same rights and obligations as nationals of the country in which they are working. These conventions also aim to maintain and protect potential rights to future benefits that migrant workers may have acquired in the country in which they work by virtue of their employment and their participation in the country's social security system. As might be expected, industrial injury benefits and old age and invalidism pensions pose the major problems.

The International Labour Organisation, founded in 1919, was concerned from the earliest years of its existence with the social insurance problems of migrant workers. It was not, however, until 1962 that an instrument applicable to the whole realm of social security (namely, Convention 118) provided equal treatment in the matter of social security. The convention made it incumbent upon member states to treat foreign nationals in the same way as their own nationals, subject to the proviso that entitlement to noncontributory benefits may be made conditional upon the fulfillment of minimum residence qualifications.

Two further multilateral instruments are of particular importance to Austria, namely the European Convention on Social Security and the convention with West Germany, Liechtenstein, and Switzerland.

On December 14, 1972, the European Convention on Social Security and a supplementary agreement were signed by Austria. Austria was, in fact, the first country to ratify the convention and the agreement. The convention and the agreement went into effect March 1, 1977. By 1983 the two treaties covered relations between Austria, Luxemburg, the Netherlands, Turkey, and Portugal.

The convention applies to the following contingencies and benefits: sickness, maternity, invalidism, old age, survivors' benefits, benefits in the case of industrial injuries and diseases, death grants, unemployment benefits, and family allowances. It is applicable to all branches of social insurance in operation in Austria. On an individual level, it applies to the nationals of the contracting parties and to political refugees and stateless persons resident within contracting parties, as well as to dependents and survivors. The principle of nondiscrimination is central to the convention: any person to whom the convention applies must be treated in the same way as the nationals of any other contracting party. The usual exception for noncontributory benefits applies—they may be made conditional upon the fulfillment of minimum residential qualifications.

The convention also addresses the transfer of cash benefits granted on the grounds of reduced or lost working capacity, old age, death, and industrial disease. The size of pension due to a claimant under the law of contracting parties where the claimant has completed insurance periods is established *pro rata temporis*.

The second multilateral convention, between West Germany, Liechtenstein, Austria, and Switzerland, was signed on December 9, 1977, and went into effect on November 1, 1980. It recognizes the high degree of labor mobility among the four German-speaking territories, particularly in the border regions. The most pressing problems in cases where a worker moves from one country to another are connected with industrial injury and pension insurance. Bilateral arrangements between any two of the four countries proved inadequate to deal with these problems. Thus the multilateral convention combines the bilateral conventions into a system that at once integrates and transcends them without seeking to abrogate them.

The convention relates to pension insurance within the meaning of Austrian social insurance law—that is, it deals with old age, invalidism, and survivors' benefits—and applies to the nationals of the contracting parties, to resident political refugees and stateless persons, and to dependents and survivors. When an insured person has completed insurance periods in two or more of the contracting parties, these periods are aggregated for the purpose of determining benefit entitlement. The amount of benefit payable by each contracting party is calculated *pro rata temporis*. The clause in the convention providing for the aggregation of insurance periods in effect extends arrangements in each of the six bilateral conventions to the whole four-country area. It ensures that no legally relevant period in any of the four countries will be "lost" as far as the acquisition, maintenance, or revival of the right to benefits is concerned.

6

◊

FUTURE AUSTRIA

PREDICTIONS ALWAYS INVOLVE SOME UNCERTAINTY, but we can point to four problems that Austria will certainly have to tackle in the coming years. The country's economic prospects are none too favorable. Like almost all industrialized countries, Austria has to prepare for reduced economic development or even economic stagnation and, consequently, for a higher rate of unemployment. In 1984 the social partners were estimating that unemployment would rise to 7 percent by 1988. Moderate in comparison with unemployment in many other countries, this level would be more than double the usual Austrian rate of 2 to 3 percent and would pose severe challenges. Judging that the economic crisis would be short-lived, the Austrian government relied on traditional Keynesian means for a solution, expanding the national budget. Known as "diving through," this policy has been hindered by an alarming rise in state indebtedness over the last few years. Structural changes in policy, including a reduction in state expenditures, have to be adopted.

In the long run, Austria will have to face drastic changes in the structure of her population. A permanent decline in the birth rate combined with rising life expectancy will result in a dramatic aging of the population, peaking in about the year 2030. The temporary rise in the birth rate that followed the withdrawal of Allied troops in 1955 and ended in 1963 will, however, temporarily ease the problem up to the year 2000; but then there will be a particularly rapid rise in the ratio of the elderly to total population. Estimates made in 1979 based solely on demographic changes concluded that in 1988 there will be 380 pensioners for every 1,000 insured persons, increasing to a maximum of 614 pensioners for every 1,000 insured in the year 2032 (see table 6.1). Yet even these estimates now seem optimistic. The Ministry of Social Affairs produced figures in July 1984 showing that, as a result of economic changes, the ratio in 1990—before the "baby boomers" reach retirement age—will be 624 pensioners for every 1,000 insured (see table 6.2). New demographic estimates underline the trend (see table 6.3). From 1990 to 2030, the number of persons over sixty is estimated to increase by 685,000, and during the same period the number of people between the ages of fifteen and sixty is estimated to decrease by 785,000. In other words, whereas in 1990 there will be 326 old people for every 1,000 persons of employable age, this ratio is expected to rise to 560 in 2030.

One might have expected the baby boom to ameliorate the financial status of the old age pension insurance system, at least over the short

TABLE 6.1
Demography of Austria,
1979 Projections (in thousands)

Year	Population	Age 20–59	Age 60 +	Ratio[a]
1975	7,295	3,501	1,526	436
1990	7,174	3,967	1,408	355
2000	7,066	3,968	1,359	343
2010[b]	6,861	3,859	1,424	369
2020[b]	6,588	3,646	1,510	414
2030[b]	6,210	3,192	1,691	530
2040[b]	5,741	2,995	1,535	513

Source: Theodor Tomandl, ed., *Finanzierungsprobleme der oesterreichischen Sozialversicherung* (Vienna: Jupiter for the Institut fuer angewandte Sozial- und Wirtschaftsforschung, 1979), pp. 54.

Notes: a. Number of people over 60 years per 1,000 people between 20 and 59 years old.

b. Numbers for these years are based on straight-line projections without measures to raise the birth rate.

TABLE 6.2

Proportion of Workers to
Old Age Pensioners,
1984 Projections

Year	Old Age Pensioners (as percentage of insured persons)
1975[a]	50.4%
1980[a]	52.7
1985[b]	59.0
1990[b]	62.4

Source: Estimates provided by the Austrian Ministry for Social Affairs, Vienna, July 1984.

Notes: a. Actual figures.
       b. Estimated figures.

and medium runs. This has not happened, however, nor is it likely to happen, because of the overall economic situation.

All industrialized countries, Austria included, will have to address the economic and social consequences of new technology. The use of computers even in small businesses, the widening application of microelectronics (especially in offices), and the introduction of robots into factories will strongly influence the employment picture as well as working conditions.

Last but not least, there are strong indications that Austria's political structure is changing. The traditional political parties are losing their reputation as efficient instruments for solving difficult social and economic problems, and the process is quickening as the parties try to expand their influence to almost all branches of modern life. Leading

TABLE 6.3

Demography of Austria,
1984 Projections

Year	Population	Age 15–59	Age 60+	Ratio*
1990	7,579	4,698	1,532	326
2000	7,625	4,685	1,566	334
2010	7,556	4,615	1,733	375
2020	7,442	4,380	1,921	438
2030	7,182	3,913	2,190	560

Source: Oesterreichisches Statistisches Zentralamt

Note: * Number of people over sixty years per 1,000 people between fifteen and fifty-nine years old.

party figures are surrounded by personal intrigue, and some are suspected of immorality and corruption. The Socialist party, which has been in power since 1970, is suffering particularly. Since Bruno Kreisky retired, no leading party functionary has been able to attract non-Socialist voters and at the same time to integrate the party's different factions. Many observers believe that the two main parties will come to resemble each other more and more and that the traditional Austrian system is being transformed into a new system greatly resembling the American one. The small Freedom party, currently in a coalition with the Socialist party, will, many believe, be squeezed out and lose its seats in Parliament in the course of the next several elections.

As environmental concerns spread among Austrians, the so-called Green Movement is become more important. The Greens belong to very different ideological camps, ranging from extreme leftists to simple nature lovers, but they are able to cooperate on occasion to thwart hydroelectric projects, nuclear power stations, new road construction, and so forth. In some provincial parliaments and local governments the Greens have already gained seats, suggesting that in national elections they may eventually supercede the Freedom party in the federal Parliament. Nor are the Greens the only novel political force making their presence felt in Austria. The importance of organized women has also been increasing. As a rule, women organize along traditional party lines, but on occasion they form ad hoc coalitions beyond partisan lines. Their organizations as a rule represent the interests of women in paid employment; the interests of homemakers are represented by less politically significant family organizations.

RISING UNEMPLOYMENT

How will economic crisis, the changing structure of the population, new technologies, and changes in the political scenery influence the Austrian social system? We believe that the main problem will be the rising rate of unemployment. Austria has not had this problem for decades. Since it became apparent that "diving through" would not work, the country has had difficulty developing efficient responses to joblessness. Many people cannot find a job after finishing their education, and about one-quarter of the unemployed are under twenty-five years of age. Older workers who have lost their jobs have almost no hope of finding new ones. The ratio of those not yet or no longer working to the whole population is rising, and this part of the population is neither formally nor informally represented by the traditional professional organizations.

The trade unions shoulder the bulk of the difficulties that arise from this development. If the unions develop strategies to achieve advantages for their paying members, who are employed, they worsen the situation of the unemployed. To try to help the unemployed, they have to gain the solidarity of their members. The dilemma is revealed most starkly in discussions about cutting the workweek. The unions aim to cut the workweek from forty to thirty-five hours. The unions view such a reduction in working hours as an efficient way of diminishing unemployment by redistributing work (a view many economists question). The major issue is whether workers will earn the same wages for thirty-five hours as they earned for forty. This is the unions' goal—that employers pay the price of the redistribution of work. The likely consequence is, however, clear. If the unions succeed, employers will have to raise productivity, and they will do so by reducing the number of jobs. Given the overall economic context, fired workers could hardly expect to find new jobs. A workweek policy addressing the needs of the unemployed therefore has to include at least a partial wage sacrifice as a signal of solidarity.

What will happen in the coming years? There is no indication of open industrial warfare. Beyond Austria's borders, in the Federal Republic of Germany, the metalworkers' union organized a vehement strike from May 14 to July 4, 1984, to enforce the immediate introduction of a thirty-five hour workweek with no wage reduction. After forty-seven days of strike the dispute was resolved by a compromise (a reduction of the workweek to 38.5 hours beginning in April 1985, combined with some wage sacrifice) that public opinion regarded as a defeat for the union. Within Austria, however, such extreme measures are unlikely. It is true, however, that the country's trade unions disagree over tactics. Alfred Dallinger, chairman of the largest union (white-collar workers) and at the same time minister for social affairs, is the most important advocate of a thirty-five-hour week to be achieved as soon as possible and if necessary by legislation. On the other hand, Anton Benya, president and most powerful individual within the Austrian Federation of Trade Unions, wants to rely on collective bargaining to achieve the shorter week more gradually. The dispute sparked discussion at the 1983 general assembly of the federation. The assembly eventually expressed no formal opinion but directed the governing board to develop a suitable strategy. According to assembly vote, the governing body will recognize international developments and try to achieve reductions in working hours by collective bargaining, mainly in those industries where unemployment is high. This assembly vote was widely understood as a victory for Benya's evolutionary tactics.

One collective agreement has already been reached, on June 20, 1984, reducing the work week in the printing industry to thirty-eight hours as of April 1985. A partial wage sacrifice accompanies the reduction: in factories that reduce their work hours, the normal wage increase provided by the collective agreement for April 1985 will be cut by 2.5 percent. That is, if a collective agreement raises the wages of printing workers by 5.0 percent, workers with a shorter workweek will receive half the nominal wage increase. The printing industry has always been something of a special case in Austria's industrial relations, as we shall show. Nevertheless, this collective agreement is likely to become a benchmark for other industries.

Legal regulations regarding hours of work are widely conceded to be too rigid. The People's party and employers' associations, in particular, favor greater flexibility. Contrary to the provisions of the legal act regulating working hours in many branches of industry, a new system has been gaining ground in the past few years. Under this flextime (*Gleitzeit*) system individual workers have more freedom to decide when to start and finish their daily work, with the proviso that each month they work all the hours for which they have contracted. Government agencies charged with implementing regulations on working hours—regulations that are still fairly rigid—have tolerated flextime and abstained from filing legal actions against the employers concerned. Flextime has generally been introduced with the cooperation of works councils; the unions, however, have some reservations about the idea.

More part-time employment, working hours distributed unevenly to match changing rates of capacity utilization (more than forty hours a week in season, fewer out of season), and even several varieties of job sharing could help ease unemployment. But for several reasons the unions do not promote such ideas. In 1983 the general assembly of the Austrian Federation of Trade Unions voted against job sharing and special variations on the idea of flextime, announcing its general opinion that flexible working hours cannot be regarded as an alternative to a shorter workweek. The unions suspect that employers will use flextime schemes to cut rather than increase employment (an additional concern is that flextime workers may prove to be more difficult to organize).

Nevertheless, while the unions attack such innovations vehemently, they appear in practice to be trying to control developments and prevent abuses rather than stopping the system altogether.

In coming years we expect a tendency to reduce the workweek by collective agreements (with or without wage sacrifices, depending on the industry concerned). This shorter workweek will probably be accompanied by increasing flexibility in the distribution of working time, a flexibility decided on a shop floor basis but tolerated and controlled by the unions.

Declining Insurance Benefits

Unemployment has a direct and adverse impact on the financing of unemployment insurance benefits. Higher contributions or higher government subsidies, or both, will be unavoidable. Indirect consequences are similarly likely in the old age pension insurance system. Unemployment reduces the number of contribution payers and increases the number of recipients of premature old age benefits. The old age pension system cannot get bigger slices of the federal budget; on the contrary, government is trying to reduce the share of subsidies destined for old age pensions.

In recent years public opinion has apparently accepted that reforms are indispensable. Political leaders first advocated cutting some benefits that appeared more or less outdated or unjustifiable in the overall context of national income. They hesitated, however, when those concerned organized resistance. The cabinet finally issued a draft covering only a small portion of initial suggestions for reform. At the same time, Alfred Dallinger deviated from his former position—namely, that there could be no further increase in contributions—and raised pension insurance contributions from 21.7 to 22.7 percent of the payroll. Between 1977 and 1985 contributions rose from 17.5 to 22.7 percent of earned wages; the financial burden of the old age pension system, in other words, has increased by 30 percent in a period of eight years. Minister Dallinger repeated his announcement that this increase in contributions would be the last for many years.

These new amendments intensify the insurance principle by modifying the pension formula. The pension will no longer be assessed on the average insured income received during the final five years preceding retirement. As noted in chapter 5, this assessment period will be extended in several steps to ten years. In the future, retiring persons will receive 1.9 percent of the assessment basis for each year of insurance up to a maximum of thirty years, and 1.5 percent for all remaining years in insurance. Older regulations, which favored insured persons with only a few years of coverage, were abrogated except for disability cases and (to a modest extent) women who have borne a child. Finally, the unemployment rate will henceforth be taken into consideration when fixing the annual adjustment of benefits. An unemployment rate above 2.5 percent will bring down the benefits coefficient, beginning in 1986. The underlying philosophy is that persons of employable age and also pensioners should share in the consequences of unemployment, stressing solidarity across society. These various modifications of the old age pensions scheme will come into effect in the course of several years. Gradual reform is a tradition in Austrian social policy, and changes in the social security system seldom occur rapidly. Normally, the legislature provides for a period of transition during which benefits or burdens are slowly raised.

The so-called pension reform of 1984, its advocates assume, will decrease the average pensions of persons who retire in the future. It is doubtful, however, that this reduction in expenses will be sufficient. Another area for potential cuts drew attention from the earliest discussion of reform: the accumulation of social benefits. Originally, benefits were reduced if a beneficiary was eligible for more than one benefit to compensate for the same deficiency. These reductions were largely repealed during the "golden age" of full employment and rapid growth. The reform debate of the last couple of years has strongly emphasized the need to reintroduce reductions in social benefits in cases where accumulated benefits seem too high in comparison with former earned income. The main beneficiaries of benefit accumulation have been widows still gainfully employed or those drawing pensions for their previous employment who also receive survivors' benefits.

The various reforms under discussion all held that women still in employment or receiving pensions of their own should cease to receive unreduced survivors' benefits. In a concerted action, women's organizations of all political and ideological orientations strongly opposed these plans. They argued that women normally earn lower wages than men and in addition have the double burden of employment and running the household. Although we believe these arguments are important, they have no significance for the system and structure of Austria's old age pensions schemes. A system that assesses pensions solely on the basis of duration of employment and amount of insured earnings cannot take into account the disadvantages that many women have to suffer. Nevertheless, the political influence that women's organizations were able to wield proved to be stronger than the logic of the system, and the government abandoned the plan. But it cannot do so permanently: persistent unemployment, budget problems, and the permanent aging of the population will require politicians to tackle this sacred cow again in future years. As soon as the finances of the old age pension system become critical again (estimates suggest this will happen in only a few years' time), discussion of the matter will have to be resumed. It will pose a particular problem for the unions, which will have to hammer out some sort of compromise between their male and female members. No political party would venture legislation on the matter without the consent of the social partners, and we doubt that any party in government would reduce the accumulation of benefits if the main opposition party opposed the idea.

Another matter concerning benefits has surfaced very recently. The old age benefit scheme for civil servants has traditionally been recognized as separate from and only peripherally connected with the general old age pension scheme. This assumption is changing. Although old age benefits for civil servants are in essence nothing more than retirement benefits that are usually financed by the employer, contributions have recently been levied and increased in line with contribution increases for the general old age pension system. This change indicates a new assessment in public opinion: old age benefits for former civil servants are no longer regarded as fundamentally different from those for workers retired from private industry. As a consequence, there is a growing demand that the principles underlying the general old age pension system be extended to the special scheme for civil servants.

Developments in 1984 illustrate the change with particular clarity. A pensioner drawing benefits from the general old age pension system suffers a reduction of benefits if he or she resumes work and earns more than a specified amount of labor-related income; retired civil servants used to be free of such limitations. In 1984 the goverment announced its intention to impose similar restrictions on retired civil servants. The reactions of the four unions representing civil servants were not unanimous. The three unions sympathizing with the governing Socialist party finally accepted the proposal under pressure from the party as well as from other unions representing workers in the private sector, which demanded equal rights for all workers. The one union sympathizing with the opposition People's party, and the party itself, strongly attacked the idea. The bill could not be passed by Parliament as the union accused the government of violating the principles of social partnership by trying to dictate terms against the express wish of a union. Negotiators were unable to find a compromise. The union threatened strike action, but the government persisted with its plan, feeling that it had wide public support. Parliament finally passed the bill with some minor changes, and the union was forced to back down.

One of the rare occasions when a union was pushed aside by a government, this event at the same time indicates the diminished reputation of public service. Public service as a whole is regarded as bureaucratic, overly large, and heavy-handed, while civil servants receive better old age and survivors' benefits than other workers. It is safe to predict that civil servants and their special benefit schemes will come under even greater pressure in the future. Austrians seem increasingly to believe that all groups within the population have to make a contribution in order to safeguard the existence of the social security system. Just as women's organizations will have a hard time defending what are regarded as unfair social privileges, so civil servants will also come under attack—and they seem to be weaker. Although they have powerful unions, public opinion does not favor public servants and is more likely to tolerate women's modest privileges in the current system.

CHANGING DIVISION OF LABOR

Young people who cannot find a job after having completed their education present a particularly important problem to Austria's economy. They cannot claim unemployment insurance benefits (of which medical coverage forms a part) because they have never been employed and hence covered in this special branch of insurance. Moreover, they cannot directly claim for sickness benefits because they are unemployed. It rests with their parents, and ultimately the public purse, to provide them with what they need, and especially with health "goods." University graduates now belong to this group, a situation almost unknown for several decades.

Young doctors leaving the universities face unusual difficulties. Newly graduated doctors need practical postgraduate training in order to be entitled to practice their profession. This training has to be given by hospitals. But training capacities, as a result of the steadily increasing numbers of medical graduates, are exhausted. Some young doctors now have to wait two or more years before being admitted to an internship. The next hurdle they face is to be admitted as a practitioner within the framework of the health insurance system. This problem may lead to modifications in training as well as in the admission system. Such changes will be achieved only by the coordinated endeavors of doctors, regional sickness funds (mainly run by representatives of the unions), and government. Likewise, we expect continuing cooperation by the state, provinces, sickness funds, and doctors to stabilize the cost explosion in hospitals. The framework for organizing this cooperation has not yet emerged, but government cannot do the reshaping unilaterally.

Automation, once a principal concern of blue-collar workers, is nowadays likewise posing problems for their white-collar counterparts, especially those working in offices. Some signs indicate that the social partners will find ways to handle the social consequences of new technologies. One demand stressed by white-collar unions is that workers be given a greater say when automation is introduced. This goal may be attained in two main ways. One is for Parliament to give workers' councils new responsibilities. With the current system of participation, we would assume that employers who plan to improve internal organization and supplant workers with machines will have to give works councils more and earlier information, discuss consequences, and eventually take disagreements to arbitration. The duty to inform, to discuss, and even to bargain about compensation for workers affected by automation already exists, but it could easily be extended.

The other way to give workers a greater say in the introduction of automation is to rely on collective bargaining and aim for collective agreements within affected industries that address the urgent problems of the industry concerned. One model is a collective agreement in the printing industry, signed in 1981. The problem centered on new methods of integrated text processing in the production of daily newspapers. The unions wanted job security for typesetters, printers, and other skilled workers whose jobs were threatened by journalists or semiskilled or unskilled clerical workers operating new machinery. The employers wanted to make full use of the new technologies. In West Germany, when the same conflict arose, the unions went on strike in February 1978, and the employers answered with a general lockout. The dispute lasted four weeks and was ended by compromise only after massive government intervention. Austria handled the problem differently. The issue was first raised in 1977 by three unions (printers, journalists, and clerical workers), which formed a bargaining unit for the purpose. The employers' association agreed to open negotiations. A moratorium was soon reached, the employers agreeing not to introduce text-processing methods until a final agreement had been signed. Negotiations were hard, and thirty-six full days of meetings finally led to a compromise. In 1981 a collective agreement was finalized, safeguarding typesetters' and printers' job security for up to ten years after the introduction of the new technology into a plant. Skilled workers who had to be transferred when the new technology was introduced could claim wage compensation. Employers were able to make this compromise because in economic terms daily newspapers are irreplaceable. Subsequent collective agreements on the issue, even in other parts of the printing industry, will have to be shaped somewhat differently. It is widely believed, however, that the social partners will find ways to reach compromises that take into consideration social issues as well as the requirements of economic competition.

Parliament's Role in Industrial Relations

Changes in technology and organization frequently reveal the relative weakness of acts of Parliament concerning labor relations. Reality is stronger than laws, especially in the shadow of unemployment. Whereas acts of Parliament tend to lose their enforcement powers over time, collective agreements between unions and employers' associations as well as shop floor agreements negotiated between workers' councils and individual employers go on setting norms that labor and management actually respect. The difference between enforcement powers of acts of Parliament and the outcomes of collective bargaining seems to lie in the greater flexibility and specificity of collective agreements. This experience is one reason why the long-term codification of Austrian labor law has not advanced for many years. At first glance, this failure may seem surprising, for one might expect a different attitude on the part of lawmakers. One reason for that expectation is that work preparatory to the issuing of new parts of the codification has long since been completed by a government commission. Another reason is political: the cabinet is obliged to show progress on a wide front to demonstrate its efficiency. In social policy, however, options are very limited because of the economic situation. The government has had to reduce public expenditures for social security. Thus activity in the field of labor law, with no direct influence on public funds, would seem to be attractive. The cabinet's apparent neglect of labor law points up, in our view, the diminishing effectiveness of state-directed labor law as well as its rigidity. Parliament, it is true, has nonetheless passed several labor law bills recently, though none are regarded as part of the codification work. This new labor legislation provides rigid rules, however, and is unlikely in practice to achieve the success that its advocates hope for.

One final development is tending to render irrelevant even collectively bargained labor law, the tendency toward a "third sector" in the economy that all industrialized countries have been experiencing for some years. "Black labor," work done on the side, and new forms of (alternative) self-employment cannot be influenced by traditional labor law, whether issued by Parliament or by the social partners. The increasing importance of this third sector, fueled by unemployment, reduced retirement age, and the unwillingness or inability of many young people to enter the formal labor market, poses a challenge for labor law as well as for the leading interest groups. They will have to find new ways of dealing with the problem. Creativity is obviously needed: today's tools, prohibitions, and administrative controls have not been successful.

The Future of the Social Partnership

The central question Austria will have to address in the near future is whether the Austrian system of social partnership will be able to handle the issues discussed so far in this chapter. The European Regional Congress of the International Industrial Relations Association, which met in Vienna in September 1984, focused its attention on the consequences of structural changes in the economy. One position met with broad acceptance: structural changes, including the permanent modernization of industry, are unavoidable. The economic and social disadvantages of delaying modernization seem to be far more serious than the consequences some industries and some workers will have to suffer as structural change occurs. The social costs of restructuring the economy can be lowered substantially, however, when government, management, and labor reach consensus. Coordinated efforts by these groups can ensure that necessary technological changes will not ignore human needs.

Austria, we argue, will be in a better position than most countries to meet these various challenges. Austrians have the institutional framework, the experience, and a settled philosophy to do so. The social partnership has been a problem-solving device from its very beginnings. It is true that in the "golden age" it was not difficult to distribute advantages, but it is also true that the groundwork for the system of social partnership was laid as Austria suffered from foreign occupation, war damage, inflation, and unemployment. It was, after all, under such extreme conditions that the mechanisms as well as the philosophy of the social partnership were developed.

We believe, therefore, that the social partnership will overcome these new challenges. A new generation, one not formed by the experience of World War II and its aftermath, is now taking up leadership positions in the government and the interest organizations. But changes in leadership have not influenced the style of Austria's social partnership in the past, and we believe that the overwhelming inclination of the Austrian population to favor the social partnership will guarantee its continuation. We do not, of course, expect an unmodified continuation. The social partnership, like any other institution, will have to adapt itself to changing conditions. It has never included all segments of the population, and groups outside the system have always struggled for recognition. Some of these groups have gained sizable amounts of power recently, and they can no longer be ignored.

Particularly notable are the workers' wing of the People's party, the Freedom party, the Green Movement, and women. Adherents of the People's party, being a minority within the trade union movement (even if much stronger than members of the Freedom party), have little say in the unions and as a consequence in the social partnership. Their best chance has always been to influence the People's party policy in their capacity as the party's workers' wing. As long as the People's party was in power, they could exercise a certain degree of influence through the government within the framework of the social partnership. When the People's party left government to become the opposition, this option disappeared. Party members now have to wield influence within the Socialist-dominated trade union movement or through the People's party within the employers' associations (which are part of the partnership system and closely connected to the People's party). The situation of the Freedom party members is even worse. Their opportunity came when the Freedom party became the partner of the Socialists in government. Now they can try to influence cabinet policy, but they still have no footing in labor-market organizations.

The Green Movement developed outside the traditional parties and interest groups. It is not even a membership-based organization; rather, it organizes people in campaigns, mostly on a regional level, on issues concerning pollution. The movement looks for public support and tries to infiltrate the traditional political parties and labor-market organizations. It has no direct access to the machinery of the social partnership, but to the extent that it succeeds in mobilizing sizable numbers of voters, the social partners and government have to take note of its goals. The situation of women is not dissimilar. There have always been special women's factions within the political parties and unions. Traditionally they have had little influence, because only a small number of women (mostly working women) worked through them. Hand in hand with the changing role of women in society and the economy, and a rising proportion of women in the work force, the importance of women's organizations has grown. They have become a power that can be disregarded no longer. Yet women's organizations as such still have no recognized position in the social partnership system, though women are strongly affected by the system.

The institutional framework of social partnership currently excludes these new forces from direct participation in decision making. We believe that in the future it will have to let them participate in some way. Presently, the partners seem to show more awareness of the demands raised by these groups than of the groups themselves. But we doubt that this reaction will be enough; some observers, indeed, have advocated a decentralization of the system, giving more individuals or collectives a chance to participate. It is, however, not clear how this can be done except by infringing on the central principles of the system: voluntary cooperation, based on mutual recognition of all participating organizations, that strictly adheres to the principle of decisions by consensus.

At present, there is no alternative to the social partnership. Most observers believe that the system will meet the problems of the near future. Such, at least, is the conviction of the vast majority of Austrian citizens, who rely far more on the social partners than on political parties to solve serious economic and social problems. The reason for their enduring commitment to the system was never more clearly expressed than by Alfons Gorbach in his farewell speech as prime minister in July 1982. In that speech he characterized the leading concepts of the Austrian system in these terms:

> Only a man with principles understands that his partner has his own principles.
>
> Only a man who is able to draw an ultimate border line is capable of recognizing the border lines his partner is unable to ignore.
>
> And only opponents who have principles and who tolerate principles will avoid going at each other with unlimited and excessive demands. Only they will find the common border line and the common way.

FURTHER READING

The Political Context

Fischer, Heinz, ed. *Das politische System Oesterreichs.* Vienna: Europa, 1974.

Nassmacher, Karl Heinz. *Das oesterreichische Regierungssystem.* Cologne: Westdeutscher, 1968.

Pelikan, Anton, and Manfried Welan. *Demokratie und Verfassung in Oesterreich.* Vienna: Europa, 1971.

Steiner, Kurt. *Politics in Austria.* Boston: Little, Brown, 1972.

Walter, Robert, and Heinz Mayer. *Grundriss des oesterreichischen Bundesverfassungsrechtes.* 5th ed. Vienna: Manz, 1985.

Weinzierl, Erika, and Kurt Skalnik, eds. *Oesterreich, die Zweite Republik.* Graz: Styria, 1972.

The Social Partnership

Farnleitner, Johann, and Erich Schmidt. "The Social Partnership." In *The Political Economy of Austria,* edited by S. W. Arndt. Washington, D.C.: American Enterprise Institute, 1983.

Fuerstenberg, Friedrich. "Conflict Management in the Austrian System of Social Partnership." In *Conflict Management and Industrial Relations,* edited by G. B. J. Bomers et al. Boston: Kluwer-Nijhoff, 1982.

Gerlich, Peter. "Partnership." In *Tradition and Innovation in Contemporary Austria,* edited by Kurt Steiner. Palo Alto, Calif.: SPOSS, 1982.

Klose, Alfred. *Ein Weg zur Sozialpartnerschaft.* Vienna: Geschichte und Politik, 1970.

Korinek, Karl. *Wirtschaftliche Selbstverwaltung.* Vienna: Springer, 1970.

Lachs, Thomas. *Wirtschaftspartnerschaft in Oesterreich.* Vienna: Oesterreichischer Gewerkschaftsbund, 1976.

Organization for Economic Cooperation and Development. *Integrated Social Policy: A Review of the Austrian Experience.* Paris: OECD, 1981.

Puetz, Theodor. *Verbaende und Wirtschaftspolitik in Oesterreich.* West Berlin: Duncker and Humblot, 1966.

Schoepfer, Gerald, ed. *Phaenomen Sozialpartnerschaft: Festschrift fuer Hermann Ibler.* Graz: Boehlau, 1980.

Tomandl, Theodor, and Franz Marhold. "Die Koalitionsfreiheit des Arbeitnehmers in Oesterreich." In *Die Koalitionsfreiheit des Arbeitnehmers,* edited by Hermann Mosler and Rudolf Bernhardt. West Berlin: Springer, 1980.

THE JOINT COMMISSION

Institut fuer angewandte Sozial- und Wirtschaftsforschung. *Materialien zur Sozial- und Wirtschaftsforschung.* Booklet no. 2. Vienna: Jupiter, 1966.

Marin, Bernd. *Die paritaetische Kommission.* Vienna: Internationale Publikationen, 1982.

INDUSTRIAL RELATIONS

Dungl, Franz, and Joachim Lamel. *Arbeits- und sozialrechtliche Regelungen in internationalen Vergleich.* Vienna: Signum, 1981.

Floretta, Hans; Karl Spielbuecher; and Rudolf Strasser. *Arbeitsrecht.* 2 vols. Vienna: Manz, 1984.

Mayer-Maly, Theo. *Oesterreichischer Arbeitsrecht.* Vienna: Springer, 1970.

Fuerstenberg, Friedrich. *Industrielle Arbeitsbeziehungen.* Vienna: Manz, 1975.

Schwarz, Walter, and Guenther Loeschnigg. *Arbeitsrecht.* 2d ed. Vienna: Oesterreichischer Gewerkschaftsbund, 1983.

Strasser, Rudolf; Konrad Grillberger; and Robert Rebhahn. "Austria." In *International Encyclopedia of Labour Law and Industrial Relations.* Deventer: Kluwer, 1983.

Tomandl, Theodor. *Arbeitsrecht 1.* Vienna: Braumueller, 1984.

———. "Labor Relations in the Public Sector of Austria." In *Public Employment Labor Relations: An Overview of Eleven Nations,* edited by Charles Rehmus. Ann Arbor: Institute of Labor and Industrial Relations, University of Michigan/Wayne State University, 1975.

LEGAL SOURCES ON LABOR LAW AND WORKERS' PARTICIPATION

Adametz, Wolfgang, et al. *Kommentar zum Arbeitsverfassungsgesetz.* Vienna: Wirtschaftsverlag, 1974.

FURTHER READING

Floretta, Hans, and Rudolf Strasser. *Kommentar zum Arbeitsverfassungsgesetz.* Vienna: Manz, 1974.

Weissenberg, Gerhard, and Josef Cerny. *Arbeitsverfassungsgesetz.* 2d ed. Vienna: Oesterreichischer Gewerkschaftsbund, 1978.

STRIKES AND LOCKOUTS

Seiler, Robert; Theodor Rittler; and Winfried Platzgummer. *Die strafrechtlichen Grenzen des Streiks im oeffentlichen Dienst.* Vienna: Wirtschaftsverlag, 1967.

Strasser, Rudolf, and Rudolf Reischauer. *Der Arbeitskampf.* Vienna: Manz, 1972.

Tomandl, Theodor. *Streik und Aussperrung als Mittel des Arbeitskampfes.* Vienna: Springer, 1965.

Tomandl, Theodor, and Franz Marhold. "Die Koalitionsfeiheit des Arbeitnehmers in Oesterreich." In *Die Koalitionsfreiheit des Arbeitnehmers,* edited by Hermann Mosler and Rudolf Bernhardt. West Berlin: Springer, 1980.

CLAIM ENFORCEMENT

Kapfer, Hans. *Arbeitsgerichtsgesetz.* 2d ed. Vienna: Manz, 1968.

Kuderna, Friedrich. "Schiedsverfahren und Gerichtsbarkeit: Die Durchsetzung arbeitsrechtlicher Ansprueche." In *Oesterreichische Landesberichte zum 9. Internationalen Kongress fuer das Recht der Arbeit und der Sozialen Sicherheit.* Vienna: Manz, 1978.

Stanzl, Gustav. *Arbeitsgerichtliches Verfahren.* Graz: Boehlau, 1954.

SOCIAL PROGRAMS AND INSURANCE

Andics, Helmut. *50 Jahre unseres Lebens: Oesterreichs Schicksal seit 1918.* Vienna: Molden, 1968.

Berger, Juergen. *Einfuehrung in das oesterreichische Arbeits- und Sozialrecht.* Vienna: Oesterreichische Gewerkschaftsbund, 1981.

Binder, Martin. *Das Zusammenspiel arbeits- und sozialrechtlicher Leistungsansprueche.* Vienna: Braumueller, 1980.

Burkert, Franz, ed. *Der Familienlastenausgleich.* Vienna: Eigenverlag, 1977.

Martinek, Oswin; Josef Cerny; and Josef Weidenholzer, eds. *Arbeitsmarktkonsistente Problemgruppen, Arbeitsmarkt und Arbeitsmarkt-service, Vollbeschaefttigung- das oesterreichische Modell: Festschrift fuer Gerhard Weissenberg.* Vienna: Europa, 1980.

Tomandl, Theodor. *Grundlegende Rechtsfragen der Arbeitslosenversicherung.* Vienna: Braumueller, 1981.

———. *Grundriss des oesterreichischen Sozialrechtes.* Vienna: Manz, 1980.

Tomandl, Theodor, ed. *System des oesterreichischen Sozialversicherungsrecht.* Vienna: Manz, 1980.

INDEX